There are six new HORIZON CARAVEL BOOKS published each year. The titles now available are:

American Heritage also publishes AMERICAN HERITAGE JUNIOR LIBRARY
books, a similar series on American history. The titles now available are:

A HORIZON CARAVEL BOOK

CAPTAIN COOK

AND THE SOUTH PACIFIC

By the Editors of

HORIZON MAGAZINE

Author

OLIVER WARNER

Consultant

DR. J. C. BEAGLEHOLE

Victoria University of Wellington, New Zealand

ILLUSTRATED WITH PAINTINGS, DRAWINGS,
AND MAPS OF THE PERIOD

Published by American Heritage Publishing Co., Inc.
Book Trade and Institutional Distribution by
Harper & Row

FIRST EDITION
Library of Congress Catalogue Card Number: 63–19987
© 1963 by American Heritage Publishing Co., Inc., 551 Fifth Avenue, New York 17,
New York. All rights reserved under Berne and Pan-American Copyright Conventions.

Inspired by the discoveries of Cook and the French explorer La Pérouse, an artist painted this brightly colored tableau, which he believed accurately represented typical scenes of native life in the South Pacific.

FOREWORD

In London's Trafalgar Square stand two naval monuments: one is a towering granite column topped by the statue of Admiral Horatio Nelson; the other is a dramatic, full-figure bronze of Captain James Cook (see page 147). Nelson showed that fighting ships could defend England against a hostile Europe; Cook showed that English ships of exploration could benefit mankind.

Captain Cook was a naval hero who never commanded a ship of the line. Yet people immediately recognized that his accomplishments were as important as victory at sea. In three great voyages between the years 1768 and 1779 he discovered the truth about the fabulous southern continent that had appeared in geographical works since classical times (but did not, in fact, exist); he conquered scurvy, the crippling enemy of ocean voyagers; and he demonstrated that longitude could be accurately computed by means of the new English chronometers. His voyages were an indication that man, with science, might one day become master of his physical world.

Enthusiasm for Cook was universal in the eighteenth century. At the height of the American Revolution, Benjamin Franklin sent out orders that Cook's ships should not be fired on because of the international value of the explorer's findings. Artists too responded to his genius—both those who sailed with Cook and those who stayed home, but dreamed of idyllic islands. Many of the works of these artists are brought together for the first time in the pages of this book.

Yet to present James Cook adequately, a book must encompass more than his life and times—for Cook's career was the culmination of centuries of ocean exploration. Thus, tales of the European and native travelers who preceded Cook are also included; his success can only be gauged against that background. As author Oliver Warner has written, Cook's truest memorial is the entire map of the Pacific Ocean.

THE EDITORS

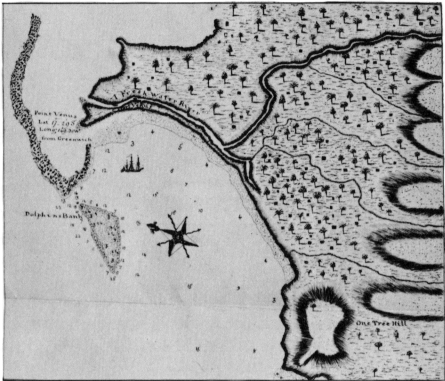

Cook's passion for detail can be seen in his chart of Tahiti's Matavai Bay, above; his artistic talent can be appreciated in the sketch of Tahiti at right.

CONTENTS

*The immense blue Pacific covers
an entire hemisphere; only a few
points in this ocean were known
before Cook's three expeditions.*

I

A NEW OCEAN

In the mid-eighteenth century, before James Cook first sailed from England, much of the world's geography was a mystery. People wondered if a habitable continent lay at the bottom of the Southern Hemisphere or if ships would ever sail over the top of the world. And geographers were eager to know the true shape of such partly explored places as New Guinea, New Zealand, and Australia. Captain Cook, in his brief but brilliant career as an explorer, succeeded in answering many of the questions posed by these mysteries. He made three spectacular voyages, sailing farther and for longer periods than any other adventurer. Yet he could not have done so without the ground-laying achievements of the dedicated and venturesome men who preceded him.

The first of these explorers was Vasco Núñez de Balboa, who journeyed across the Isthmus of Panama in 1513. The journey was not an easy one. Balboa and his Spanish companions—accompanied by a half-mile-long procession of native servants—trudged for three weeks through the cragged hills and thick forests and over the rocky streams. The terrain of the Isthmus made foot travel hazardous, but Balboa and his men eventually reached their objective. According to one contemporary account:

... on Tuesday the twenty-fifth of September of that year one thousand five hundred and thirteen, at ten o'clock in the morning, Captain Vasco Núñez, going ahead of all those he was conducting up a bare, high hill, saw from its summit the South Sea ...

It was a historic moment. The captain knelt, as did his men, to offer a prayer of thanks for being privileged to make the discovery. Then they climbed down to the beach, and Balboa, his boots lapped by the foaming surf, claimed for God and for Spain the mighty ocean he had been first to see.

Balboa's discovery touched off an epoch of exploration

that gradually filled in the blanks on the map of the newly discovered ocean. What Balboa began early in the sixteenth century was finished some 250 years later by James Cook, who did more than any other man to complete the map of Balboa's South Sea.

In the years between Balboa and Cook, men of many nations cast their gaze toward the farthest shores of this vast new ocean and probed its deepest secrets. Some men sailed in search of legendary islands or to find new trade routes to the East. Others looked for the unknown southern continent. No one had seen this land mass, but geographers were convinced it must be there—if only to balance the continents of the Northern Hemisphere.

Emboldened by her discoveries in the New World, Spain sent other explorers after Balboa. In 1519 Ferdinand Magellan sailed to the South Sea, and because of its calm waters named it the Pacific. His expedition was the first to cross this vast ocean and sail around the world, and he became known as the greatest explorer of his age.

Born in Portugal in 1480, Magellan was still in his teens when Vasco da Gama, a Portuguese mariner, opened up a sea route to the East by sailing to India. Once there, da Gama confirmed the long-held belief that India had many valuable resources, including spices. Explorers in subsequent years heard stories about a still richer source of spices—particularly cloves—that was to be found on a group of islands southeast of China. The islands were known as the Moluccas or the Spice Islands.

Magellan also heard these stories when he sailed to the East as a young naval officer. Other explorers had reached the Moluccas by sailing the long and dangerous route around the tip of Africa. Magellan came to believe that the islands might be reached by sailing west instead of east, which meant crossing first the ocean Columbus had sailed and then the one Balboa had discovered. Magellan's faith in this plan was upheld by his notion that the Pacific was only 600 miles wide. He could not have imagined that the distance from the west coast of South America to the Moluccas, even if traveled in a straight line, was 11,000 miles.

He might have offered his plan to the Portuguese king, but Magellan's outspoken nature had not endeared him to that monarch. King Manuel I despised him—so much so that when Magellan requested a promotion in the navy, the king refused and suggested that Magellan seek other employment. It was this setback that made him decide to go to Spain. In Spain he felt certain his services would be

DE BRY, *India Occidentalis*, 1590

12

*Gold and spices lured early explorers. This 1590 engraving shows Balboa
and his men fighting over tributes of gold brought to them by the natives.*

Ferdinand Magellan

appreciated—and he might receive support for his plan in the Spanish court.

He arrived in Seville in 1517 and quickly convinced King Charles V of the need for Spain to be the first nation to send ships to the Moluccas by sailing directly to the west across the uncharted seas. Magellan was given a complement of 241 men and two years' provisions, and he was promised a sizable percentage of whatever riches he discovered. Five ships were fitted out for his use. Magellan himself took command of one of the larger vessels, the 110-ton *Trinidad*, as the expedition embarked from Seville on August 10, 1519.

The Portuguese were furious. They had regarded Magellan as a mere boaster as well as a blunt and disagreeable man. Now King Manuel feared that Magellan would win for Spain what might have been Portugal's. So he ordered a small fleet of Portuguese ships to race to the Cape of Good Hope, at the southern tip of Africa, and head off Magellan's flotilla. If the captains planned to lie in wait

for the explorer, they must have been disappointed. His route took him westward across the Atlantic and then down the South American coast. He was well out of reach of the Portuguese ambush.

Magellan's ships hugged the coastline as he searched for signs of a break in the land—a strait that he hoped would lead him into the uncharted South Sea. The farther south he went the worse the weather was. The sea boiled around the ships, and angry winds punished the sails. In May, 1520, one ship, off by itself reconnoitering the coast, was wrecked on the rocky Argentine shore. A rescue party returned the nearly frozen crew to safety; no lives were lost.

By now the southern winter had struck in full force, so Magellan and his party anchored their ships in the mouth of a river and spent the next few months on land. During this period their onshore exploration yielded little except an encounter with some natives who had extraordinarily big feet and who took delight in gulping down whole rats without even bothering to skin them.

By the time of Magellan's voyage, Portuguese traders had become well established in the East Indies. Below is a sixteenth-century scene of Calicut, a port on India's west coast, crowded with trading ships.

In October, as summer approached and the ice in the river began to melt, the Spaniards returned to their ships and resumed the voyage south. Later that month a cape was sighted. It proved to be a gateway to the channel Magellan had been eager to find. Flags flew from the masts and guns boomed a salute as the ships steered into what would later be called the Strait of Magellan.

Not all the men were so enthusiastic as Magellan. Many of them declared aloud their fear of sailing into an unknown sea. Midway through the strait, one captain refused to continue. His ship was the largest, with the most stores, and perhaps he thought that if he turned back, Magellan would have to do likewise. However, left with but three ships and fewer provisions, Magellan vowed that even if they had to eat the leather wrappings on the masts and yards, he would go on.

Fortunately the weather was good. But the task of negotiating the tortuous strait, with its maze of islands and channels and its constantly shifting currents, was an arduous one. The ships proceeded cautiously. Ice-capped mountains rose from the channel on one side of them. On the other side were islands on which fires flickered constantly. The natives had not yet learned how to kindle a flame, so they kept campfires burning all the time. Magellan named the region Tierra del Fuego, "Land of Fire."

On the evening of November 28, after thirty-eight days in the twisting channel, where the tides rose and fell as much as forty feet, the ships emerged into the calm Pacific. Jubilantly the men fired salvos from the ships' guns, shattering the silence and frightening the sea birds that glided overhead. For long weeks thereafter no land was seen.

"We were three months and twenty days without getting any kind of fresh food," wrote a member of the expedition, Antonio Pigafetta, in his chronicle. "We ate biscuit which was no longer biscuit but powder of biscuits swarming with worms . . ." Pigafetta also reported, "The gums of both the lower and upper teeth of some of our men swelled, so that they could not eat under any circumstances and therefore died." The men were victims of scurvy, a vitamin-deficiency disease brought on by a lack of fresh vegetables and fruit. Seamen for centuries would be plagued by it.

After heading north, paralleling the Chilean coast for several hundred miles, the ships steered west and pushed farther and farther into the empty sea. When land was finally sighted, it proved useless to the expedition: a group

HERRERA. *Historia de los Hechos de los Castellanos,* 1728

16

The tip of South America is viewed from the Pacific side in the Spanish map below; north is to the left. Tierra del Fuego appears as a large island separated from Chile's mountainous spine by a narrow passage, the Strait of Magellan. At left is a fairly realistic drawing of Tierra del Fuegans by John Webber, one of Cook's artists.

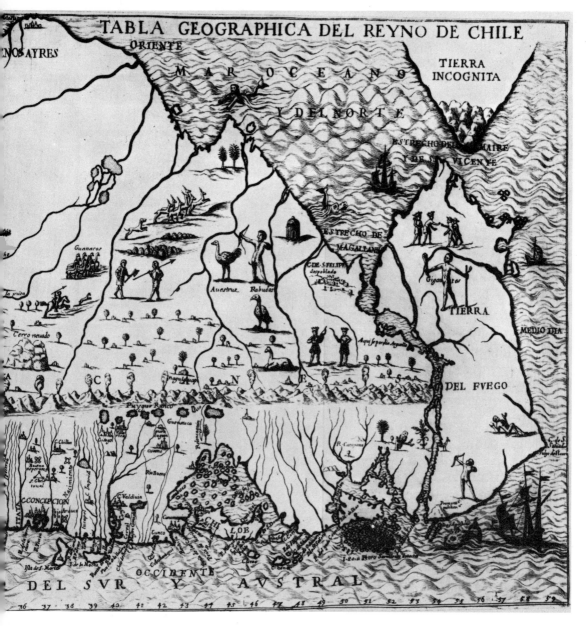

17

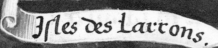

In Pigafetta's journal the Mariana Islands are called the Isles of Thieves ("Isles des Larrons").

18

of tiny islands that appeared to support no life. As the ships sailed onward the crews' hunger increased; their growing discontent became more of a threat to their commander. Finally on March 6, 1521, a mountain was seen in the distance against the horizon. The lookout who spotted it was so weary and so thirsty that his voice cracked as he cried out, "Praise God, land! Land!" Then he broke into tears.

The three ships steered toward the land, which turned out to be another island (now called Guam, one of the Marianas group). It was small, but it did have life. Fruit grew in abundance in the dense, damp forests, and fresh water flowed from the mountain streams. To Magellan and his once-dispirited crew, the island must have resembled a paradise.

The explorer hoped now to discover other islands where food and water might be found and where his ailing men could rest and recover. He continued on his westerly course until more land—the Philippines—came into view. There the sight of native chieftains wearing gold bracelets and long gold earrings convinced the Spaniards that the wealth of the East was almost in their grasp.

Magellan had not sailed the broad Pacific to colonize or to proselytize, but he could not ignore an opportunity to spread the faith by which he lived. On Easter Sunday, 1521, the Spaniards held a religious service, and curious natives who watched the proceedings were invited to embrace the Cross. Magellan was pleased that they accepted Christianity, and as he moved from island to island he developed a religious fervor that had a tinge of arrogance.

Native chiefs were accustomed to receiving tribute from their visitors; Magellan refused to offer it. He believed that as a representative of the Christian world and of Spain, then the greatest power on earth, he need not submit to a lesser authority. Not long after Easter he imposed his faith on a native rajah, district chief of a whole group of tiny islands. The rajah and the explorer then performed a ritual that made them blood brothers.

Magellan soon learned that his "brother" was troubled by the disobedience of another tribe in the district. Feeling all-powerful now, Magellan vowed that he and his men would force the dissidents to capitulate. By doing so, he thought he could prove the Christians' strength and valor and the superiority of their God. He refused the rajah's offer of reinforcements and ignored the pleas of his own men not to lead the expedition himself. On April 26, Magellan and

Off the Philippine island of Cebu ("Zzubu" on map below) is Mactan. Magellan (above) met his end there while fighting in a native war.

PIGAFETTA. *Premier Voyage Autour du Monde.* 1801

TEXT CONTINUED ON PAGE 22

19

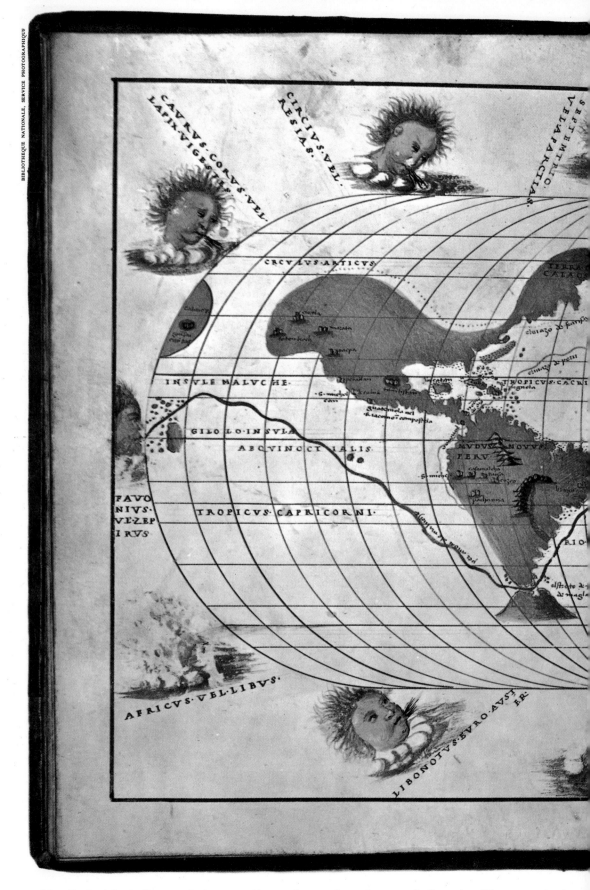

Magellan's globe-circling route is shown on this map from a sixteenth-century Italian atlas. The map maker locate

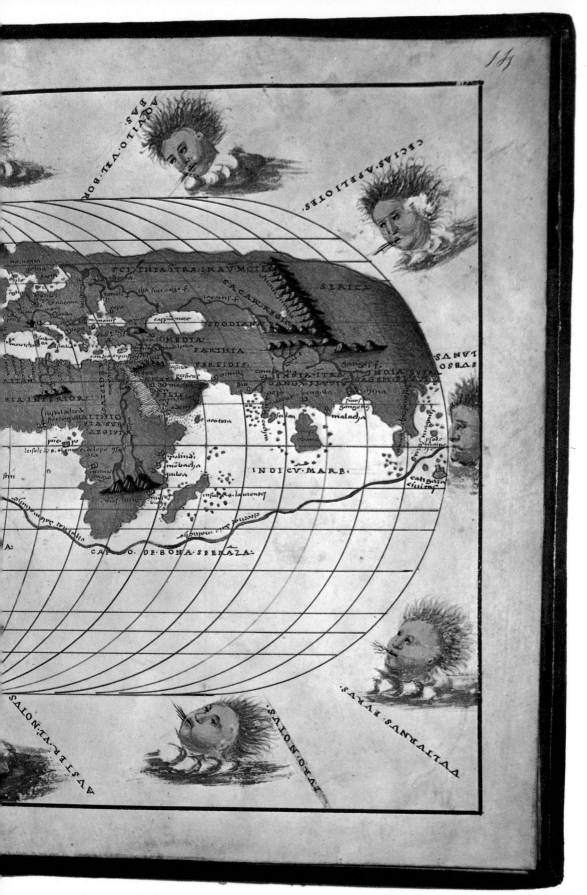

he Moluccas ("Insule Maluche"), which had been the expedition's goal, off the Asian coast (at extreme left of map).

This spirited drawing of one of Magellan's ships, the Victoria, *was made soon after the explorer's death. An angel hovers on the bow; Magellan stands on the poop deck.*

TEXT CONTINUED FROM PAGE 19

fifty armed Spaniards landed on an island called Mactan.

Hordes of natives met them on the beach, shouting and shooting great volleys of arrows. Hoping to fend off an attack, for the Spaniards were vastly outnumbered, Magellan ordered his men to burn the native huts. Pigafetta, the chronicler, reported that when the islanders "saw their houses burning, they were roused to even greater fury . . ." So many stones and spears were being hurled that the Spaniards could offer no resistance. They were helpless to do other than grope their way to the waiting boats as the natives pursued them. The chronicle continues:

Recognizing the captain, so many turned upon him that they knocked his helmet off his head twice, but he always stood firmly like a good knight . . . An Indian hurled a bamboo spear into the captain's face, but the latter immediately killed him with his lance . . . Then trying to lay hand on sword, he could draw it out but halfway because he had been wounded in the arm with a bamboo spear. When the natives saw that, they all hurled themselves upon him. One of them wounded him on the left leg with a large cutlass . . . That caused the captain to fall face downward, when immediately they rushed upon him with iron and bamboo spears and with their cutlasses until they killed our mirror, our light, our comfort, and our true guide.

Magellan was dead. The hero of the expedition was gone, but its heroic aspects were not yet over. Although the Pacific had been crossed, there was still much to test the strength and endurance of Magellan's survivors, who were still halfway around the world from home.

It took the men seven months to reach the Moluccas, where they spent several weeks trading for cloves with the natives. Then after setting a southern course through the Indian Ocean and rounding the Cape of Good Hope, the survivors reached Spain in September, 1522.

For more than two hundred years, Ferdinand Magellan's achievement stood alone as the most important feat of sea exploration. Other men—Spanish, French, Dutch, English—followed him to the Pacific, and so many determined voyagers sailed around the world that circumnavigation began to seem almost commonplace. However, more than half of the mighty ocean was as yet untraveled. No explorer had opened up as much new territory for his country as Magellan had. Not until 1769, when James Cook first reached the South Pacific, were the Portuguese-born mariner's achievements equaled—and then exceeded.

In England at the time of the first Cook voyage, a potter named Josiah Wedgwood perfected a new glazed, cream-colored earthenware to which he gave his name. Wedgwood dishes and vases soon became popular—as did medallions with relief portraits of famous national figures like Cook (right).

HONOLULU ACADEMY OF ARTS

Pall Mall Magazine, 1896

NATIONAL MARITIME MUSEUM, GREENWICH HOSPITAL COLLECTION, GREENWICH

BIBLIOTHEQUE NATIONALE, SERVICE PHOTOGRAPHIQUE

FLAGS IN THE PACIFIC

Columbus, Balboa, and Magellan were but three of the adventurous explorers sent westward by Spain at the opening of the sixteenth century. Following Magellan's route, a host of ships flying the white cross of Spain sailed into the Pacific and helped stake out the greatest land-and-sea empire the world has ever seen. When Luis Vaez de Torres sailed between Australia and New Guinea in 1606, Spanish discovery reached its climax. But during the seventeenth century, the tide of empire ran out for Spain. In Europe she found she was unable to rival England or keep the Netherlands within her grasp, and in the Pacific her flag no longer dominated. Instead, the flags of sturdy Dutch trading vessels (like the storm-rigged ships on the raging sea below) were seen with increasing frequency as the merchants of the Netherlands followed where their explorers led. Most brilliant of the Dutch explorers was Abel Janszoon Tasman (far left), who reached New Zealand in 1642. At left are three piratical-looking Englishmen who also contributed to the eclipse of Spain in the Pacific: Sir John Hawkins, Sir Francis Drake, and Thomas Cavendish. Eventually these men be-

TEXT CONTINUED ON PAGE 26

TEXT CONTINUED FROM PAGE 25

came as famous for their voyages of exploration as for their raids on Spanish ports. One of the most spectacular strikes at the riches of the declining Spanish empire was made by George Anson (left below) in 1743 when he seized a treasure-laden galleon off the Philippines and took the silver back across the Pacific to England. By that time the French had also become active in the Pacific islands, hoping to found colonies and foster trade. The first Frenchman to sail around the world was Louis Antoine de Bougainville, who is seen below waving a large flag on a small rock in the Strait of Magellan. Conflicting European plans to establish vast trading empires in the Pacific did not provoke naval battles in the centuries before Cook's voyages, but there were many bloody contests with the natives. At right below, a Polynesian sailing canoe is fired upon by Dutch explorers who are pursuing the natives in one of the ship's boats. At right above, an English explorer's ship, Samuel Wallis' *Dolphin*, is attacked by native canoes in Tahiti in 1767. Despite local incidents and international rivalries, the explorers who preceded Cook were able to bring back to the capitals of Europe enough information to begin filling in the puzzling map of the Pacific Ocean (see overleaf).

ANDERSON, *Captain Cook's Travels . . . , 1784*

The Ladrones (left), now called the Marianas, were touched upon by Magellan and sighted by Spain's Pedro de Quirós.

New Guinea's north coast was reconnoitered by the Englishman William Dampier in 1699.

A passage between New Guinea ("Nouvelle Guinee") and Australia ("Nouvelle Hollande") was navigated by the Spaniard Luis Vaez de Torres in 1606.

Many of the islands north of New Zealand ("Terre des Estats") were explored by Louis Antoine de Bougainville on his global voyage of 1766–69.

Having sailed south of Australia (left), Abel Tasman discovered Tasmania (below) and New Zealand (right) in 1642. But he never knew their actual geographic relationship.

The South Indian Ocean bordering on the Pacific was investigated in 1722 by Yves de Kerguélen, who hoped to find a southern continent for France.

The Pacific was a puzzle of isolated coasts and inexactly charted islands before Cook voyaged there in 1768. T

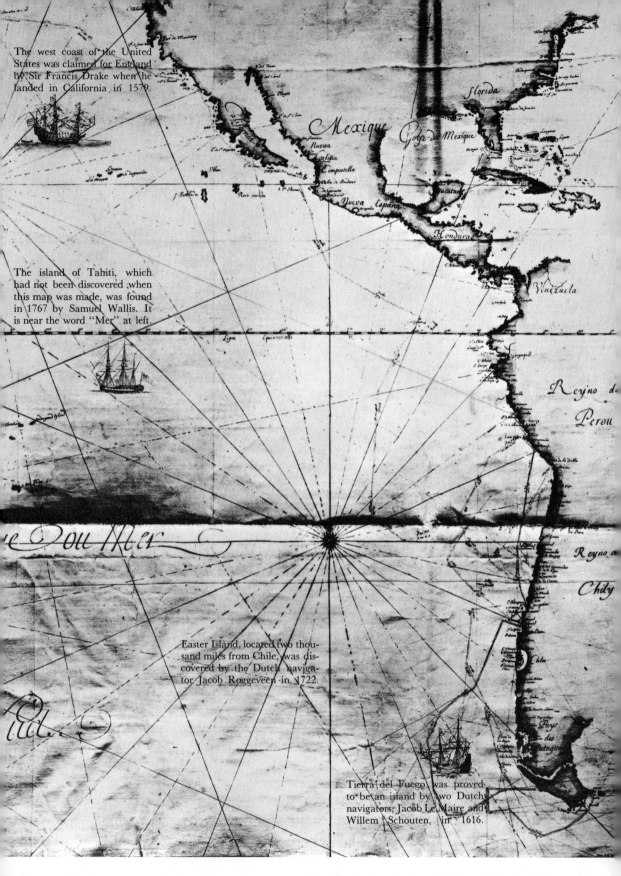

The west coast of the United States was claimed for England by Sir Francis Drake when he landed in California in 1579.

The island of Tahiti, which had not been discovered when this map was made, was found in 1767 by Samuel Wallis. It is near the word "Mer" at left.

Easter Island, located two thousand miles from Chile, was discovered by the Dutch navigator Jacob Roggeveen in 1722.

Tierra del Fuego was proved to be an island by two Dutch navigators, Jacob Le Maire and Willem Schouten, in 1616.

Major events of South Seas exploration between Magellan and Cook are indicated on this 1711 French map.

II

THE MAP MAKER

James Cook once described himself as a man "who had ambition not only to go farther than anyone had done before but as far as possible for man to go . . ." These words not only sum up his professional aspirations but also give a rare, personal glimpse of the man himself, for Cook was an individual endowed with a special, piercing curiosity. He had few of the characteristics of a visionary seafarer like his great predecessor Magellan. Cook was a methodical explorer with the soul of a scientist, and he was born into an age when the search for scientific knowledge was as intense as the thirst for conquest had once been.

By the 1700's, England had established an impressive sea tradition, and her people had shown themselves to be good colonizers. She was reaching out now to all the unclaimed regions of the world, eager to expand her realm of trade. The eighteenth century, the age of reason and enlightenment, required a new kind of explorer: not a rover or a plunderer, or a seeker of adventure for its own sake. The desire for geographic discovery was foremost. In addition to being a master of navigation and seamanship, an explorer was expected to be a highly skilled surveyor and chart maker. And besides having a natural curiosity, he was expected to have a strong flair for command.

Cook was exactly the kind of man that was needed; otherwise he could not have succeeded as he did. His experiences prior to his three great voyages shaped his determination, and most important, gave him the strength to face hardship and the will to endure.

He was born on October 27, 1728, in a two-room clay cottage in the remote Yorkshire village of Marton. His

In the 1780 portrait at left, James Cook is pictured as a well-tailored and severely handsome naval officer. The two English sailors at right, both wearing cutlasses, are typical of the "jack-tars" who sailed with Cook.

31

father, a day laborer, worked hard for the welfare of his seven children. James proved a bright youngster. Because of the promise he showed, his father's employer financed his early schooling in Ayton, near the farm on which the elder Cook worked. After leaving school, young James assisted in the farm work, and then his father found him a job with a shopkeeper in Staithes, a tiny fishing village northwest of Whitby. Here the boy was to learn a retail trade.

At Staithes, within sight of ships sailing to and from the nearby port of Whitby, and within earshot of surf pounding the rocky shore, Cook developed a love for the sea that was to last a lifetime. In summer, at every opportunity, he was on the water. In winter, when the boats were tied up, he took it upon himself to learn as much as he could about the shipwright's craft.

Eighteen months passed. By then Cook's preference for seafaring was obvious to everyone—even to his employer,

Whitby, where James Cook served his apprenticeship, still retains much of its eighteenth-century character. Above is the present-day Whitby harbor front; at right is the graceful doorway of the house of Cook's employers.

The location of Whitby can be seen on the 1744 map below—above the word "Yorkshire" on England's North Sea ("Noort Zee") coast. On this stormy sea, Cook sailed bluff-bowed colliers like the ship at far right. From the ship's waist, men are unloading coal into a barge. The sketch of Cook at right shows a sober young man with a white wig and a three-cornered hat.

COOKE, *Shipping and Craft*, 1829

who graciously arranged for him to secure an apprenticeship with a shipping firm owned by John and Henry
Walker. The Walker brothers' home port was the seacoast
town of Whitby.

The Walkers were prominent coal shippers. Their business was to run coal-carrying vessels, called colliers, between London and the Yorkshire towns along the North
Sea coast. Whitby was at that time a coastal-trade center
as well as an important shipbuilding site, so it was easy
enough for a seventeen-year-old like James Cook to fulfill
the desire to roam. He learned to handle the awkward but
capable colliers and sail them safely in dangerous waters.
He served nine years in the North Sea trade—first as an
apprentice, then an able seaman, and finally as a mate.
During the last three years he was second-in-command
of his ship.

This was a valuable experience, primarily because it
taught him to trust his instinct. In those days even the
coastal charts were unreliable. A seaman had to have a
sixth sense to protect his ship from shoals, sandbanks, and
changes of current. Cook was unusually perceptive in his
youth. And in later years he gained a reputation for being
a man who would sail where other navigators dared not go;
he seemed to know instinctively which waters were safest.
His officers often said that he could smell land, relating how

35

he would appear suddenly on deck and alter his ship's course when no one else was aware that she was in danger of running aground.

Cook served the Walkers of Whitby so well that in 1755 he was offered command of one of their colliers. But he turned down the offer. He was nearly twenty-seven and he wanted a change. England and France were being drawn closer to what was to be the Seven Years' War. Now England was mobilizing. Her navy was so short of men that scouting parties were sent into the streets and taverns of waterfront towns in search of recruits.

Cook recognized the need for experienced seamen and at the same time foresaw the possibility of advancing his career at sea. So he enlisted as an ordinary sailor on one of King George II's warships. Five weeks after being assigned to the *Eagle*, his first ship, he was promoted. Now he was master's mate, primarily responsible, under his captain, for navigating the ship and also for keeping a log.

Serving in a ship the size of the 60-gun *Eagle* could offer splendid training for a young man eager to learn the business of navigating and scientific surveying. Just how much he learned would be determined in part by how much he was allowed to do. And he was fortunate to have a new

TEXT CONTINUED ON PAGE 41

When he first entered the navy, Cook served under Captain Hugh Palliser (left), who was an experienced officer and a keen Admiralty politician. Cook's first battle was in 1758 in the siege at Louisbourg (below) when the English took from the French the easternmost and best-fortified citadel in North America.

The French believed that the English fleet could not sail up the St. Lawrence from Louisbourg to assault Quebec. But Cook's accurate charts, drawn under constant threat from cannon batteries above the river, enabled

the fleet to proceed upriver. In this print, English infantrymen scramble out of their landing craft and up a narrow defile to the wooded heights. The final battle was fought on the Plains of Abraham (left background).

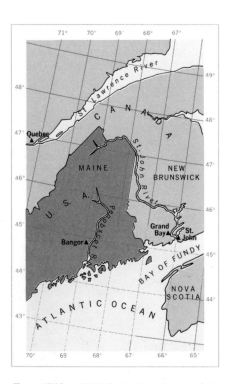

From 1762 to 1769 Cook charted much of the east coast of Canada. A portion of one of his charts from this period is at right. It shows the southern course of the St. John River below the arm that swings north and west to form a part of the boundary of New Brunswick and Maine (see the present-day map above). Near the mouth of the St. John River, Cook drew in a stubby sea monster.

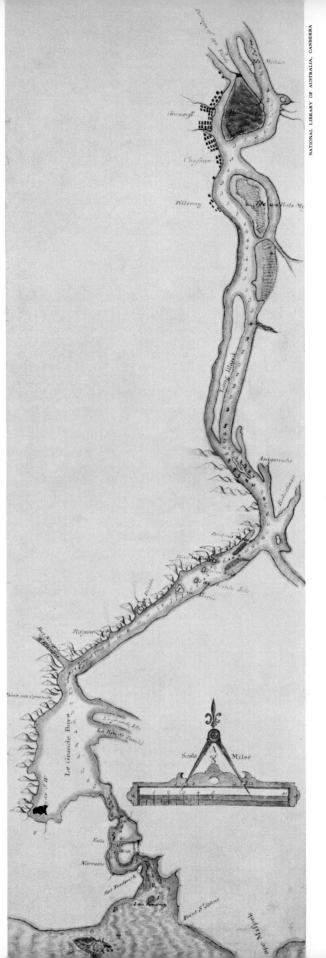

TEXT CONTINUED FROM PAGE 36

captain take command of the ship only four months after he himself came aboard. Captain Hugh Palliser, an experienced officer and a wise judge of character, quickly recognized Cook's abilities and eventually became the young man's patron and friend.

Cook served aboard the *Eagle* for two years after war between France and England had broken out. He was promoted again in 1757—this time to master. His ship was the *Pembroke*, assigned to North American waters. The fleet she joined was to take part in the siege of Louisbourg, a fortress on the eastern tip of Nova Scotia.

The English considered Louisbourg a strategic objective, for it commanded the Gulf of St. Lawrence at the mouth of the river. While the French held Louisbourg no attack on the capital of New France—the city of Quebec—was possible. So on June 7, 1758, an English infantry force was led ashore to assault the fortress. A choppy sea made the landing difficult, and many soldiers were drowned in the effort. Still others were slaughtered by the raking French gunfire. But the English would not be turned back. On July 26, 1758, Louisbourg fell.

Now there was only one deterrent to an attack on Quebec. The St. Lawrence River, as it narrowed toward the city, was choked with shoals and dangerous reefs. Cook and the masters of a few other vessels were asked to chart a suitable channel. If their work proved accurate, the English fleet could be piloted through the channel and anchored opposite the city.

This was extremely hazardous duty for Cook and his men. Much of the time they made their soundings under the noses of the French, for Quebec's main fortifications stood atop an enormous promontory that overlooked the channel. Cook went about his work calmly and efficiently, even though the threat of death or capture was literally hanging over his head. When the charting was finished, after many months, the English fleet safely entered the channel, and the Battle of Quebec began.

After more than six weeks of fighting, the city surrendered to the English. Now Cook could undertake his first important piece of independent work: a detailed survey of the St. Lawrence River from Quebec to the Atlantic Ocean. Cook's meticulous charts made the earlier ones obsolete and firmly established his reputation as a skilled marine surveyor.

Back in England in 1762, Cook felt secure enough in his career to venture into marriage. His choice of a wife was

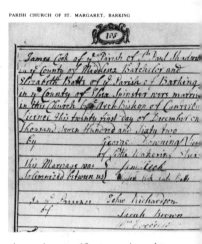

PARISH CHURCH OF ST. MARGARET, BARKING

A marriage certificate was issued to James Cook and Elizabeth Batts in December, 1762, "by ye Arch Bishop of Canterbury's licence."

41

Elizabeth Batts, a London girl who was thirteen years his junior. He found her a house east of the busy heart of London—a house that was rarely a home for him but mostly a place in which to rest between voyages. Elizabeth was an aloof and reticent person like her husband. She was aware that the nature of his work required long periods of absence from England. She accepted her role as a continually abandoned wife with grace and resolution; she was her husband's own sort.

Only a few months after his marriage, Cook was off to North America again to survey the unknown Newfoundland coast. Some time later his former captain, Palliser, became governor of Newfoundland and arranged for Cook to command a series of chart-making expeditions in Labrador as well as Newfoundland. During the next five years he spent the winters in England completing his charts, and in the summers he worked busily to learn the secrets of the dangerous coasts over which Palliser had authority.

The noted geographer Alexander Dalrymple seemed a likely choice to lead a South Pacific expedition.

From his work on these coasts he became well known among responsible naval men. And from those who served under him came his reputation as an efficient, dedicated, yet coldly scientific individual. He was a man of rigid standards, and never a man to cross. His temperament was made even more volatile by the lingering pain of an accident he suffered on a charting expedition. A powder horn exploded in his hand and all but severed his right thumb. Though he was nearly deprived of the use of his hand, the precision with which he did his work was unmarred. His charts of Newfoundland and Labrador were so accurate that they were not wholly superseded until late in the nineteenth century. And his detailed report of an eclipse of the sun, which he observed in 1766, enhanced his reputation as a scientist. Thus it was logical that the Royal Society, England's leading scientific body, should become interested in Cook. A mission was being planned that only a seaman-scientist of Cook's caliber could handle.

After the coronation of King George III in 1760, England had become interested again in geographical discovery. Unlike a number of his predecessors, the new king preferred to extend his imperial authority through exploration rather than through conquest. He had sent several ex-

The Admiralty decided that the best ship for Pacific exploration would be a Whitby bark. Cook was familiar with these ruggedly built coast-wise vessels (left); as captain, his quarters were in the stern (beneath the flag).

plorers to the South Pacific—among them Captain Samuel Wallis, who had discovered Tahiti in 1767.

To many, the selection of James Cook as Wallis' successor was a surprising move. Most people thought a true scientist would head the next expedition to the Pacific. And there was no scientist with a more valid claim to lead such an expedition than Alexander Dalrymple, who had been a lifelong student of geography and surveying. At this time Dalrymple was preparing a manuscript outlining his theory that a southern continent not only existed but extended well north into temperate climates. Because of his scientific interest in the South Pacific, it is logical to suppose that he too expected to be offered an expedition to command.

But Admiralty policy had changed. In the past, and with disastrous results, civilians had failed to exercise strong leadership when given positions of authority at sea. Now it was specified that only a naval officer with wide experience could lead an expedition, and that the scientists given passage aboard ship should have no responsibilities other than to their work. Cook met the prerequisite. The expedition he was asked to command had two missions, the first of which was strictly scientific.

Earlier in the century the astronomer Edmund Halley had predicted that in the year 1769 the planet Venus would pass between the earth and the sun. If this phenomenon, called the transit of Venus, were accurately observed, it might be possible, astronomers said, to calculate the exact distance between the earth and the sun. A committee of the Royal Society suggested that the transit be observed from

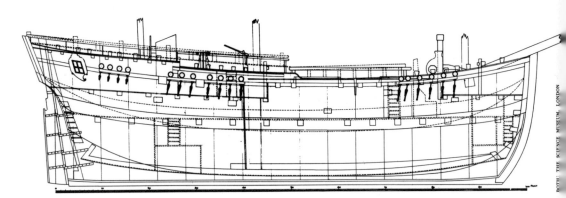

Cook's first expedition was in the Endeavour, *a 106-foot bark whose details have been reconstructed in the scale model at right. Note the square bow with gun ports. The plan above shows that the vessel was roomy but not deep; she was sufficiently shoal of draft to venture into uncharted waters.*

Two famous natural scientists accompanied Cook on his first voyage: Joseph Banks and Dr. Daniel Solander. Banks (left) possessed adequate reputation and funds to have his portrait done by Sir Joshua Reynolds, the fashionable society artist. Solander, one of England's ablest botanists, is seen opposite in an engraving from a 1772 London journal.

three different vantage points—to check and double check the calculations. The sites suggested were Hudson Bay, North Cape (northernmost point of Europe), and an unnamed spot in the South Pacific. Captain Wallis' effusive descriptions of Tahiti made this island the logical choice.

Cook's primary mission, then, was to observe from Tahiti the transit of Venus. His second objective was a secret and was contained in sealed orders which Cook could not open until after the astronomical phase of the expedition had been completed. He was fairly certain, however, that he would be asked to perform some feat of exploration.

Dalrymple, deeply resentful of having been passed over, rejected the offer to sail with Cook as chief scientific observer of the transit of Venus. Imperiously he replied that he would certainly observe the astronomical phenomenon from wherever he happened to be, but that he would go to the South Pacific only if he were given command responsibilities.

By this time Cook was already preparing for the voyage. A vessel had been purchased and fitted out precisely for his purpose. She was named the *Endeavour* and was of a build with which Cook was thoroughly familiar. He had served his apprenticeship on a north-country collier just like her, and she had actually been built at Whitby.

The *Endeavour* was a roomy, deep-waisted vessel whose broad, flattened bow tapered toward a square stern. She was a strong ship, and from her figurehead to the tip of her stern she measured 105 feet. Cook once said of her, "In such a vessel an able sea officer will be more venturesome and better enabled to fulfill his instructions than he possibly can in one of any other sort or size."

On May 27, 1768, two days after he had been promoted to the rank of lieutenant, Cook took charge of his ship. Three months later, on August 26, the *Endeavour* set sail from Plymouth. Aboard, in addition to her complement of officers and sailors, she carried a number of scientists. There was an astronomer, Charles Green, and a noted botanist, Dr. Daniel Solander. But the man whose impact would be most felt was Joseph Banks.

At twenty-five, Banks was fifteen years younger than Cook and already a recognized botanist. He had inherited a large fortune, which made him independent and helped him gratify his wide-ranging curiosity. He had sailed to Newfoundland and was eager now to explore the uncharted regions of the Southern Hemisphere. He traveled royally —always with a retinue of scientific helpers, artists, and servants.

Just as Cook desired recognition as a professional mariner and outstanding explorer, Banks hoped to be lauded by both the social world and the world of learned men. The success of the expedition was as important to one man as to the other, but for different reasons. The two became fast friends despite the difference in their ages and temperaments—possibly because of Banks' extreme tact and Cook's unwavering authority.

The expedition's first port of call was the island of Madeira, four hundred miles from Africa's northwest coast. Here Cook distributed a large quantity of fresh onions among his men; his fight against scurvy had already started. The *Endeavour* continued south and then crossed the Atlantic to Rio de Janeiro, where Cook intended to replenish his supply of food and water. He met with unexpected difficulty there, however, for the Portuguese governor was anything but hospitable. He could not believe that the *Endeavour* was a naval vessel and was convinced that

The London Magazine, 1772

Dr. Daniel Solander

her crew was involved in smuggling. Cook and the ship's surgeon were the only men allowed ashore to bargain for provisions, and then only under the eyes of an armed guard.

In January the *Endeavour* reached Tierra del Fuego, and some of her crew disembarked to look for wood and water. While the ship rode at anchor in the icy Bay of Success, Banks and a scientific party, with some servants and seamen, climbed up the green hills that overlooked the water. The climb took longer than they had calculated, and before they could get down, darkness and a bitter snowstorm overtook them. Banks forced them to keep going, weary as they were. He knew the dangers of stopping to rest in the extreme cold. Two of the servants did not heed his advice. They lay down exhausted in the snow and died during the night. The other men barely escaped death. Only Banks' unyielding spirit—and a vulture that he shot and cooked over a fire at breakfast time—kept them alive until they could return to the ship.

Resuming her voyage, the *Endeavour* had a relatively easy passage around Cape Horn. She escaped the terrifying gales that were usually encountered in these waters. On January 30, 1769, she reached latitude 60°10', her "farthest south," and then followed a northwesterly course toward Tahiti (see end sheets). Ever since leaving Cape Horn, Cook had been militant in enforcing the dietary rules he knew would prevent scurvy. He had collected berries and greens—the so-called scurvy grass—at Tierra del Fuego, and he succeeded in having his men eat the sauerkraut brought from England; it was healthful, brimming with vitamins, and bitter as brine—hardly the kind of food that hearty seamen would enjoy eating. An entry from Cook's journal indicates how they were persuaded to do so:

Men at first would not eat until I put into practice a method I never once knew to fail with seamen, and this was to have some of [the sauerkraut] dressed every day for the cabin table, and permitted all the officers without exception to make use of it and left it to the option of the men either to take as much as they pleased or none at all. But this practice was not continued above a week before I found it necessary to put everyone on board on an allowance [strict ration], for such are the tempers . . . of seamen in general that whatever you give them out of the common way, although it be ever so much for their good . . . you will hear nothing but murmurings against the man that first invented it; but the moment they see their superiors set a value upon it, it becomes the finest stuff in the world and the inventor an honest fellow.

NATIONAL MARITIME MUSEUM, GREENWICH

Before leaving for the Pacific, the Endeavour *was fitted out in the dockyards at Deptford. This view of Deptford in 1778 shows the launching of a 74-gun ship.*

On April 13, 1769, the *Endeavour* anchored in Matavai Bay on the north side of Tahiti. Cook had reached the haven that had so bedazzled Captain Wallis. He soon found that his predecessor's enthusiasm had been justified, for the island seemed every bit as idyllic as Wallis had described.

Wallis had reported that metal of any kind was precious to the Tahitians, for they had none, and that any favor might be purchased with a common iron nail. Immediately after the *Endeavour* had anchored, Cook issued a set of regulations to his crew. These were indicative of his attitude toward any dealings to be made with people of the islands

49

Most of the existing scenes of the first voyage were drawn by Sydney Parkinson, who had joined Cook as a botanical draftsman. His sketch of the Endeavour *in a rough sea is at right. Below is Parkinson's wash drawing of Matavai Bay in Tahiti, the first Pacific landfall.*

View of the Bahs of Orowhaina in the Bay of Matavai. Otaheite.

he would visit. He stated first that he wished "by every fair means to cultivate a friendship with the natives and to treat them with all imaginable humanity." And he insisted that "no sort of iron or anything that is made of iron, or any sort of cloth or other useful or necessary articles are to be given in exchange for anything but provisions." Cook had not come to Tahiti to exploit the natives; he made that clear.

Soon after the ship was secured, Cook and the intrepid Banks went ashore along with officers who had visited the island two years earlier with Wallis. Cook was eager to find a good site from which to observe the transit of Venus, and he was relieved to find, upon reaching the island, that the Tahitians were as friendly and cheerful as Wallis had reported. As soon as the natives recognized familiar faces among the new arrivals, they called out "*taio, taio*" ("friend, friend") and overwhelmed the Englishmen with gifts of fruit and flowers, pigs and fowl.

The Tahitians were a beautiful brown-skinned people who spent their days swimming and fishing under the balmy skies. They were a hardy people—equally adept at wrestling as at swimming and dancing. They dressed in cloth made from the hammered-out bark of trees and were fond of wearing flowers in their hair. Women as well as men were tattooed with geometrical designs, the result of a painful operation done with a sharpened bone covered with a sooty liquid.

The natives were clean, cordial, and hospitable, but Cook wrote in his journal that they had one disagreeable tendency: ". . . they are thieves to a man and would steal but everything that came in their way and that with such dexterity as would shame the most noted pickpockets in Europe." Thieving was one of their chief pursuits as well as their chief skill. Dr. Solander lost his opera glasses on his first day ashore, and the ship's surgeon lost his snuffbox. Once after a feast, Cook spent the night ashore and took the precaution of hiding his stockings under his pillow. He need not have bothered; in the morning they were gone.

The most brazen act of thievery occurred when a musket was snatched from one of Cook's sentries. Another guard fired on the thief and killed him. This was a highly provocative act, but the Tahitians seemed satisfied that the culprit had deserved punishment, and they remained friendly to Cook.

The expedition's most serious loss was its quadrant, an instrument by which the officers computed the *Endeavour*'s position. Banks, breathless with rage, hiked some four miles

This portrait of Sydney Parkinson was done by an unknown artist.

into the island's interior to retrieve the valuable object, but he found it in pieces. The natives, eager to possess every metal article they could find, had taken the instrument apart. It was finally put back together, but it never worked properly again.

June 3 was a cloudless day on Tahiti; the transit of Venus was clearly observed and the calculations were carefully recorded. Unfortunately, the results proved useless. Venus is perpetually shrouded by a cloud zone; thus the planet cannot be used for accurate observational purposes. Cook did not realize it, but he was no more or less successful in his observation than scientists in other parts of the world.

Successful or not, Cook had done as he had been directed. Now the first phase of his expedition was over. A sealed envelope contained the information he had waited many months to read—orders that spelled out his destiny.

Cook's chart of the double island of Tahiti ("Otaheite") shows the location of Matavai Bay and Point Venus, both on the north side (bottom) of the island's larger half.

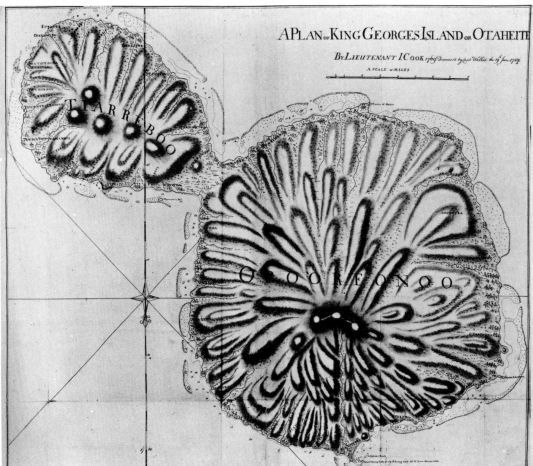

A Plan of King Georges Island or Otaheite

By Lieutenant J Cook 1769 Discovered by Capt Wallis the 19 June 1767

A SCALE of MILES

T ARREBOO

O TOOREONOO

An English water-colorist, George Tobin, painted this picture of himself being carried in full dress across the foaming Matavai River in 1792.

III

SECRET ORDERS

"You are to proceed to the southward . . . until you arrive in the latitude of 40°, unless you sooner fall in with [the southern continent] . . ." This is how a part of Cook's sealed instructions read. Another part stated that if he did not reach land by latitude 40°, he was to go westward to New Zealand and learn whether it was part of a larger land mass, the unknown southern continent.

New Zealand had been discovered, but only partly explored, by the Dutch mariner Abel Janszoon Tasman in 1642. His expedition had been the first ever to sail south of Australia, thus ending the suspicion that Australia might be connected to the long-sought continent. However, no one knew the geographical limits of New Zealand, for Tasman had mapped only its western shore. The geographer Dalrymple was certain New Zealand was a peninsula that extended north from the mysterious continent. Cook's job now was to prove or disprove this theory.

The nature of Cook's secret instructions was hardly a surprise to him. Rather, he would have been surprised if his mission had consisted simply of the journey to Tahiti. Before fulfilling this more adventuresome phase of the expedition, Cook decided to have the *Endeavour* "careened." She was run ashore and tilted by means of ropes and winches attached to her masthead. Then the bottom of her hull was scraped clean of any plant or sea life that clung to it. Cook was happy to see that his ship had suffered no damage; only a coat of pitch was needed to seal her wood surfaces against leaks.

After a three-month stay, the *Endeavour* left Tahiti. She took with her a man named Tupaia who had been one of the island's principal priests. He had learned some

PARKINSON, *Journal of a Voyage* . . . , 1773

Spear-wielding Australian aborigines (right), and warriors like the top-knotted Maori above, were among the gravest threats on Cook's first voyage.

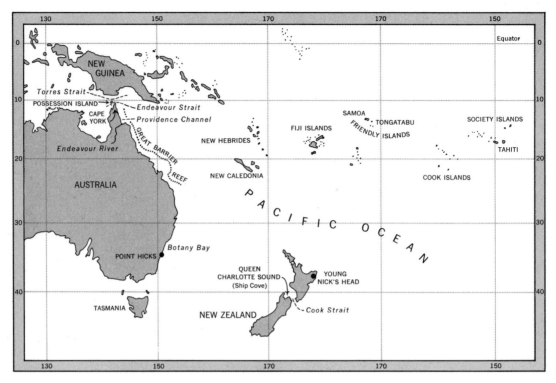

Equator

NEW GUINEA

Torres Strait
POSSESSION ISLAND
CAPE YORK
Endeavour Strait
Providence Channel
Endeavour River
GREAT BARRIER
REEF

SAMOA
TONGATABU
FRIENDLY ISLANDS
SOCIETY ISLANDS
FIJI ISLANDS
TAHITI

NEW HEBRIDES

AUSTRALIA

NEW CALEDONIA
COOK ISLANDS

PACIFIC OCEAN

POINT HICKS
Botany Bay

QUEEN CHARLOTTE SOUND
(Ship Cove)
YOUNG NICK'S HEAD

TASMANIA

NEW ZEALAND
Cook Strait

English and was eager to travel. Cook believed Tupaia would prove useful as an interpreter when the expedition visited other islands nearby. Cook named these the Society Islands, for he noted that they "lay contiguous to one another." On August 9 Cook set his course to the south, and the *Endeavour* nosed into uncharted waters. Everything that came into view now would be new; everything would require description and interpretation. Never was precise observation more necessary.

Cook pressed on for nearly a month, rolling through choppy seas and fighting high winds that damaged the *Endeavour*'s sails and rigging, but no continent came into sight. A heavy swell from the south suggested that there could be no land for a long distance in that direction. The southern continent, if it existed at all, obviously did not extend into the temperate latitudes—at least not in that part of the Pacific.

When Cook reached latitude 40° 20′, which was slightly beyond the limit prescribed by his instructions, he changed to a westerly course. Now he was heading toward New Zealand, whose eastern shores had never been seen.

Late in September, after following a zigzag course—

From the green island of Tahiti Cook sailed south and then west to New Zealand's unexplored islands, where eventually he found a good harbor at Queen Charlotte Sound. In 1770 he started home, but not before he had charted the perilous east coast of Australia.

ANDERSON, *Captain Cook's Travels . . .*, 1784

first northwest and then southwest—Cook saw seaweed floating around his ship. He knew land could not be far away. At two in the afternoon of October 7, 1769, Nicholas Young, the boy at the masthead, shouted, "Land ahead!" He thus won the gallon of rum offered to the first crew member to sight land. The ship at this time was not far off New Zealand's North Island—a point on the east coast that was later named Young Nick's Head.

As Cook's men on the *Endeavour* were soon to learn, they had not reached a particularly hospitable part of the land. The coastline did not offer many suitable harbors, and when they made their first landing they found that the native Maoris were quite unfriendly. Although the people understood Tupaia as he spoke to them, they were otherwise dissimilar to the amiable Tahitians. The Maoris frequently paddled out to inspect the *Endeavour*. Often they would trade, always driving a hard bargain, but sometimes, even without provocation, they would toss stones and darts at the startled Englishmen.

Firing over their heads did not make the natives less quarrelsome or more obliging. Cook learned this lesson one day when he ordered his men to discharge their muskets. The Maoris reacted so violently that the Englishmen had to shoot to kill in order to protect themselves.

No matter what they did, no matter how well meaning they were in these first encounters, Cook and his men were regarded with suspicion and hostility. The simple gifts that had delighted the Tahitians held no fascination for the New Zealanders. They desired only weapons of war.

Little initial progress was made in establishing rapport

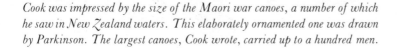

Cook was impressed by the size of the Maori war canoes, a number of which he saw in New Zealand waters. This elaborately ornamented one was drawn by Parkinson. The largest canoes, Cook wrote, carried up to a hundred men.

On the sixteenth-century map at left, Asia (top) was drawn with rough accuracy down through its southeastern peninsula. But the land mass pictured farther south and called Jave La Grande was purely conjectural. Cook eventually proved it did not exist. He started out by showing that New Zealand was not part of such a continent—that it was in fact two islands divided by the strait at right now named after Cook.

with these Maoris, but Cook made considerable progress in exploration. He cruised northward and rounded New Zealand's uppermost tip. Then he sailed down her west coast until he reached a thirty-mile inlet that he named Queen Charlotte Sound. Here he found a snug and beautiful little bay where he spent a month having the *Endeavour* cleaned again. He called this bay Ship Cove.

While the *Endeavour* was being worked on, her officers reconnoitered the surrounding country, poking through woodlands and cutting through thickets. One day Cook and a sailor climbed a hill to try to see what lay beyond the inlet where their ship had found a haven. Peering eastward, they realized that Queen Charlotte Sound opened into a strait that separated two bodies of land.

This strait was given Cook's name; his discovery proved that at least one part of New Zealand was an island. He was later convinced by a friendly Maori that the other part was also an island. When the *Endeavour* was ready to sail again, Cook went through the strait—back to the east coast —and set out to circumnavigate this southern island.

Many of his officers still believed New Zealand to be an appendage of the elusive southern continent. But by mid-March, when the *Endeavour* had negotiated the storm-tossed waters at the southern tip of New Zealand and was making her way up the west coast, everyone had changed his mind. Even Banks, a staunch supporter of Dalrymple's theory, had to concede later that he had seen "the total destruction of our aerial fabric called continent." On March 24 Cook found himself once more in the strait that bore his name; his circumnavigation was completed. As proof of this achievement he had accurate drawings—the first ever—of New Zealand's two main islands.

TEXT CONTINUED ON PAGE 62

The self-sufficient Maoris showed no interest in trading or communicating with the men of Cook's expedition. This nineteenth-century print shows a Maori scene—a few grass-covered huts and two magnificent dugout canoes.

BRITISH MUSEUM OF NATURAL HISTORY

The men of the *Endeavour*, the scientists as well as the officers and seamen, were growing homesick. Cook felt justified in turning back now, in view of the number of charts he had drawn and of the new discoveries they recorded. Although he had not seen the unknown continent, or disproved its existence, he decided to break off the search. He wrote in his journal: ". . . as to a southern continent, I do not believe any such thing exists unless in a high latitude [near the South Pole] . . ." The next day he sailed out of New Zealand waters.

Cook's orders gave him the freedom to choose his own homeward route, as he was by this time about halfway around the world from England. If he sailed home eastward, around Cape Horn, he might prove or disprove the existence of a continent lying south of his outward route. Sailing west, by way of the Cape of Good Hope, would permit him no such advantage. However, the *Endeavour* was in no condition for a long, arduous cruise in the icy southern seas. So Cook decided to sail west after all and make a stop in Australia. After scouting her still uncharted east coast, he would continue westward until he reached the colony of Batavia in Java. Here further refitting could be carried out, if necessary, and the ship's stores could be replenished for the homeward voyage.

At dawn on April 19, 1770, a landfall on Australia was made. One of Cook's lieutenants sighted a long, low section of coastline that was eventually named Point Hicks after him. Cook turned north. As the wind was favorable, he held to this course until, on April 28, he found a sheltered bay in which the *Endeavour* could be anchored. He called this inlet Sting Ray Harbor because it had an abundance of the large, flat fish whose barbed spines made them so fearsome. The shore of Sting Ray Harbor had a wealth of plant life that eventually engaged Banks and Solander so completely that Cook felt compelled to change the name of the inlet to Botany Bay, a name it still bears.

As the *Endeavour* worked her way into the harbor, some natives were seen spearing fish from a canoe. They displayed no interest in the vessel, which must have seemed enormous as she floated toward them with her towering spread of canvas. A few of them came onto the beach as Cook and Banks brought a landing party ashore. Try as they might, the white men were unable to communicate with these Australian aborigines, and Tupaia's calls in his native Tahitian brought no reply. The Australians just wanted to be left alone.

Australia fascinated the expedition's naturalists with its many unknown plants and strange animals. They had never seen the animal at left, for instance, a kangaroo sketched by Parkinson. Another specimen is examined by two men in the painting below as Cook claims the land around them for England. Cook explains in the log at right that the many new varieties of plants in this region led him to name the inlet where they anchored Botany Bay.

63

The Englishmen, on the other hand, were fascinated by the dark-skinned natives whose bodies were painted with broad, white streaks. The sailors were most interested in native weaponry, although they did not understand it; they thought at first that the boomerang was a curved wooden sword.

Cook left Botany Bay on May 7 and sailed along a thousand miles of uncharted shore during the next five weeks. After he had crossed the Tropic of Capricorn, on his way north, navigation through the coastal waters became more difficult—and then downright dangerous. The inshore waters were unnavigable because of shoals, and not far out to sea lay a hazard of nature of which Cook was unaware, the Great Barrier Reef.

This massive reef is the largest coral deposit in the world. The southern tip of the reef lies about 150 miles offshore. It runs northwestward for more than 1,200 miles, converging steadily toward the Australian east coast. Cook could not have known he was approaching a death trap as he kept sailing north, but he was aware that there were obstacles dotting his course. He urged his lookouts to remain vigilant at their posts. And because of the unevenness of the ocean floor, he continually took soundings with the "lead line" used for that purpose.

On June 11 the depths became extremely irregular, alternating sharply between deep valleys and steep hills of coral rising from the ocean floor. Toward evening, however, an area of consistently deep water seemed to have been reached. There was a smooth sea and a bright moon. Instead of anchoring for the night, Cook took the considerable risk of sailing on under reduced canvas. Then he went below deck for a well-earned rest.

Just before eleven o'clock, as the *Endeavour* was stealing along at the rate of one knot, the soundings showed a depth of about seventeen fathoms. Then, before another sounding could be made, the ship struck hard and remained stuck on a ledge of coral. One of the two great crises of the voyage had occurred.

Recounting the event later, Banks told a friend that Cook "was upon deck in his drawers as the second blow was struck, and he gave his orders with his wonted coolness

THE MUSEUM OF PRIMITIVE ART, N.Y.

The Australian aborigines used small boomerangs like the two-foot weapons above for sport. Larger ones that did not fly in a circle were used for war. The aborigines also made artistic objects like the bark painting at right.

and precision." The *Endeavour* was thirty miles from land, and there were not enough boats to take all the crew off should the ship have to be abandoned. Banks had heard stories of how a crew could easily be thrown into a panic in times of acute danger; therefore he was impressed, he said, by "the cool and steady conduct of the officers, who, during the whole time, never gave an order which did not show them to be perfectly composed and unmoved by the circumstances, however dreadful they might appear." As for the seamen, they "worked with surprising cheerfulness and alacrity; no grumbling or growling was to be heard throughout the ship, no, not even an oath . . ."

There was a procedure to meet such emergencies at sea, one that had been formulated after centuries of bad—and often tragic—experiences. Sail was taken in. Boats were hoisted out to take soundings all around the ship and to trace the lie of the reef. Anchors were then lowered from the *Endeavour* in the hope that she might be hauled off by pulling on the anchor cables. At the same time the crew

Below are the Endeavour*'s small boats, drawn by Parkinson. They were used mainly for landings and sometimes to tow the ship in calm weather. After the* Endeavour*'s mishap, the boats went out to explore the coral ridge now known as Australia's Great Barrier Reef.*

Composed of the skeletons of marine animals solidified into rock-hard masses, coral reefs throughout history have been a menace to ships in tropical seas. Above is a photograph showing varieties of coral.

worked speedily to lighten the ship in every way possible. Spars were struck down and shoved overboard, and fresh water, firewood, six irreplaceable guns, and forty or fifty tons of stone and iron ballast were jettisoned into the sea.

The *Endeavour* had struck at the peak of the high water, and the lightening process took several hours to complete. Meanwhile, the tide was falling. When the ship was finally ready to be hauled off the reef, the tide had fallen four feet —fully enough to nullify all the work that had been done. The men had to wait until high water came again.

But when the tide rose, nothing could be accomplished. Despite her loss of weight, no heaving on the cables would budge the *Endeavour*. But the next high tide, which occurred after nightfall, was slightly more pronounced. With a lurch, the ship floated free—to be hauled clear and anchored in deep water. Here her spars were replaced. Then she was taken ashore where the damage to her hull was surveyed.

A chunk of jagged coral had punctured the hull. The resulting leak was serious; the pumps could gain on the flow of water gushing into the ship only after tremendous effort on the part of all hands. Better results were obtained from "fothering" her, a process that Cook described in his journal:

The manner this is done is thus: we mix oakum and wool together (but oakum alone would do) and chop it up small and then stick it loosely by handfuls all over the sail and throw over it sheeps' dung or other filth. . . . The sail thus prepared is hauled under

Beached on the shore of the river named for her, the Endeavour *is inspected and readied for repairs. Her equipment is laid out nearby.*

68

the ship's bottom by ropes, and if the place of the leak is uncertain it must be hauled from one part of her bottom to another
until the place is found where it takes effect; while the sail is
under the ship, the oakum etc. is washed off and part of it carried
along with the water into the leak and in part stops up the hole.

After the ship had been patched in this manner, one
pump alone could cope with the flow of water, and the men
at last could reduce their labors. Cook now found an inlet,
the mouth of the Endeavour River. It was extremely narrow but deep enough so a ship could float close to shore.
He guided her across a sand bar with perhaps only inches
to spare. In this accomplishment lay a major justification

HAWKESWORTH, *Account of Voyages* . . . , 1773

for having chosen a collier-type vessel with a shallow hull. No regular man-of-war or deep-built merchantman could have been brought in safely.

On further inspection it was discovered that the damage had been nearly fatal to the ship, for the coral had sliced cleanly through the bottom and cut away four planks. The largest opening was filled by a piece of coral that had broken off and remained stuck in the gap. This helped considerably to lessen the leak.

Repairing the ship caused the expedition's longest stay on the Australian mainland, for the *Endeavour* was not fit to sail again for about six weeks. Banks and Solander bustled about, collecting botanical specimens. And the crew had time to roam, hike, and hunt leisurely. Not much in the way of edible foodstuff was found growing—a few palm cabbages and some pulpy fruit called plantains—however, fish, turtles, and oysters were caught in abundance along the shore. And Cook and his men became the first Englishmen to see such peculiarly Australian creatures as the kangaroo, the wallaby, and the dingo.

During this stay on the shore, another attempt was made to communicate with the natives, but they turned out

On his way home, Cook stopped at Java, a Dutch-held island. The drawing above, done shortly after his visit, shows the Javanese port of Surabaya. Cook also stopped at the Dutch East Indies port of Batavia. The desolate fort in the old painting at right was probably an island outpost near Batavia.

70

to be as aloof as their fellow tribesmen had been at Botany Bay, Cook's first landing. They refused the trinkets that were presented as peace offerings. And when they were not allowed to carry off turtles the English had captured, they lighted a grass fire to try to burn down the explorers' tents and the linen that was hanging out to dry.

When the *Endeavour* was ready for sea again, early in August, Cook decided he would have to take her outside the Great Barrier Reef. He feared that the reef would converge still closer to the mainland and the ship would be trapped. He sent his sailing master out in a pinnace to sound the depths. Then he himself climbed a hill to look out for patches of troubled sea. ". . . I saw that we were surrounded on every side with shoals," he wrote, "and no such thing as a passage to sea but through the winding channels between them . . ."

Cook managed to get through the dangerous passage out between the shoals, but then before he had attained the necessary sea room beyond the reef, the wind dropped. The danger now was more acute than before, for the *Endeavour* was being driven by the swell toward the reef. If she were to hit it, she would be shattered.

The boyhood home of Cook is now a national monument in Melbourne, Australia. Originally in York-shire, it was dismantled in 1933, shipped in pieces to Australia, and reconstructed, vines and all.

Because of the water's unfathomable depth, no anchor could be used effectively to hold the ship back, so she drifted relentlessly onward. Then when she was less than a hundred yards from destruction, Cook sighted an opening in the reef—Providence Channel he rightly called it. Her boats managed to tow the *Endeavour* toward the gap, and she was swept through swiftly. The second crisis was over.

Within the reef once again, Cook was determined to continue northward, whatever the consequences might be. He wished to verify the existence of a navigable strait separating Australia from New Guinea. This was the strait that Luis Vaez de Torres claimed to have discovered in the seventeenth century (see map on page 56).

Making further surveys by boat, Cook learned that it was possible after all to work his way up the coast inside the reef. On August 21 he reached the northern promontory of Australia, which he named Cape York. On that date too he sighted the mouth of the channel between Australia and New Guinea. Torres' discovery could no longer be doubted.

Now that Cook had achieved his objectives, he felt free

to return home to England. Before leaving the land that he was never again to see, Cook made a landing on what came to be called Possession Island. It was here, in the fading light of a tropical sunset, that he took possession of the entire east coast of Australia—two thousand miles of which he had surveyed and charted in the previous four months. As the British flag was run up, the landing party fired their muskets. This salute was answered by the ship anchored close to the shore. The ceremony was one of thanksgiving as well as of triumph.

Under way once again, Cook now set a westerly course, groping with great care through the channel that he called Endeavour Strait. This passage was south of the one Torres had found on his voyage in 1606. Cook reached Batavia on October 10, 1770, and had his ship overhauled. She was ready for sailing in a month, but he was delayed until December 26 because of illness among his men.

The stay in Batavia proved more injurious to health than any other phase of the expedition. The colony was rife with malaria and dysentery, and though the men arrived there healthy, there was soon a long sick list. A great many deaths occurred at Batavia and at other stops along the last leg of the voyage. Among the fatalities were Green the astronomer, the artist Sydney Parkinson, the surgeon, and even poor Tupaia, the Tahitian adventurer who had taken passage to see the world.

The *Endeavour* carried fifty-six of her original ninety-four men when she anchored in the English Channel on July 13, 1771, after a slow journey around the Cape of Good Hope. Cook was received with acclaim by the public, the Admiralty, and also King George III. He wrote proudly to John Walker of Whitby: ". . . I had the honor of an hour's conference with the King the other day, who was pleased to express approbation of my conduct in terms which were exceedingly pleasing to me."

In an exhaustive report to the Admiralty, Cook offered his own modest judgment that the discoveries made on the voyage were not great. However, in terms of the distance he had sailed and the five thousand miles of coastline he had charted, his voyage was the greatest yet made by an explorer. And further, he had mapped with a precision that until then was unknown. He was promoted to the rank of commander, and within weeks after presenting his report, he was at work on new plans. He had unlocked many secrets of the great South Sea, but as far as he was concerned, a great many still remained.

King George III warmly welcomed Cook upon his return home. Above is a caricature of the king; below is a statuette of the captain.

IV

SEARCH FOR A CONTINENT

After James Cook's triumphal return to England there could be no doubt that a second expedition to the South Pacific would be organized—and that Cook would be asked to lead it. There were other persuasive factors in addition to Cook's proven fitness as a commander and his eagerness for further exploration. Hugh Palliser, Cook's early patron, was now a man of influence on the Navy Board; the geographer Dalrymple was still unconvinced that the entire existence of his "balancing" continent had been disproved; and Banks was as enthusiastic as Cook to sail once more.

English pride had much to gain from another voyage, for France was redoubling her activity in the field of exploration, and Spain was showing some worry about English voyages in the Pacific. It was essential that England

The Resolution *unfurls her sails and heads seaward at the center of this fanciful harbor scene. The* Adventure, *which also sailed with Cook on his second voyage in 1772, has been painted from two different angles (at far right and far left).*

challenge her rivals and maintain her hard-won supremacy.

By early 1772 it had been decided that Cook should sail with two ships instead of one. Recalling his frightening experiences along the Great Barrier Reef, Cook could easily see the wisdom of having a consort—as a backstop against the danger of shipwreck or other sea disaster. The *Endeavour* had been more than satisfactory, but as she was now on a routine voyage to the Falklands, two newly constructed Whitby vessels were purchased for Cook. One was larger and the other was smaller than the *Endeavour*. They were named the *Resolution* and the *Adventure*.

The *Resolution*, the larger of the two, was to be Cook's own ship for the rest of his life. She had a crew of 110 men, many of whom had sailed with Cook before. The second vessel, carrying 80 men, was commanded by Lieutenant Tobias Furneaux, who had sailed around the world with Captain Wallis.

The expedition had a rather difficult beginning, the cause of which could be traced to Banks. He lavished great sums of money on preparations for the voyage and recruited a retinue of twelve men—scientists, draftsmen, servants, and a portrait painter—to accompany him. As the *Resolution* did not have room for these extra passengers, a new deck was built at the waist of the vessel. Even Cook's quarters were appropriated, so a new captain's cabin had to be constructed. Banks entertained expansively aboard the vessel, but he was not to sail on her.

When the *Resolution* was finally fitted out to meet the botanist's exacting demands, one of Cook's most reliable officers, Charles Clerke, told Banks: "By God, I'll go to sea in a grog-tub, if required, or in the *Resolution* as soon as you please, but must say I think her by far the most unsafe ship I ever saw or heard of." In Clerke's view she was top-heavy, and his opinion was shared by the Board of Admiralty and by every shipwright who knew his business. Cook himself was convinced that he could not sail in the *Resolution* until she had been restored to her former well-balanced state.

Banks, of course, was livid. He withdrew his retinue and his baggage from Cook's expedition and went instead to Iceland. It speaks much for Cook's character that he never allowed this ugly incident to mar his respect for Banks. Although Cook may have regarded Banks' withdrawal as the removal of a minor irritation, he was soon to regard the absence of Dr. Solander, the naturalist, as a major loss. Solander had been one of Banks' cronies and did not rejoin the Cook expedition. Instead the Admiralty sent

DE VARGAS MACHUCA, *Milicia y Descripcion de las Indias*, 1599

At the bottom of this 1599 globe lies the fabled southern continent whose existence Cook was finally to disprove on his second voyage.

two Germans, Johann Reinhold Forster·and his son Georg. Each was skilled in natural science and botany, and though Georg was admired by everyone, his father was a peevish sort who proved tiresome early in the voyage.

Banks originally had planned to include the famous German-born portrait artist John Zoffany on the expedition, but when Banks withdrew, so did Zoffany. William Hodges was substituted. He was a landscape painter with a delightful sense of light and color, but he shared certain illusions of his time about the "noble savage." Although he saw the South Sea Islanders with his own eyes, his paintings were more romantic than realistic—and furthered a myth, then popular in Europe, of the carefree savage living an idyllic existence.

Next to Cook, the commander, the most important members of the expedition were a pair of astronomers, William Wales in the *Resolution* and William Bayly in the *Adventure*. They would fulfill one of the expedition's major functions—improving and refining the means of determining longitude. They were to be aided in their work by an instrument called a chronometer.

For centuries mariners had known how ·to calculate latitude, their north-south position at sea. But as they never knew the exact time, they could not figure out accurately how far east or west they were. The first marine timekeepers, controlled by pendulums, were fashioned in the late seventeenth century. They were not particularly accurate, for their mechanisms did not function well in the changing temperatures experienced at sea.

Early in the eighteenth century a one-time carpenter named John Harrison finished what was to become the first reliable seagoing clock. It was spring-driven and was remarkably accurate—the result of Harrison's ability to compensate for fluctuating temperatures. He accomplished this by using many different metals to vary the spring tension. His clock would keep accurate track of the time at zero degrees longitude no matter where the instrument was taken. Knowing the time at zero degrees (site of the Royal Observatory at Greenwich, England) a navigator could use his sextant and astronomical tables to determine local time wherever he was. Then by converting the difference between local time and Greenwich time from hours to degrees (one hour equals fifteen degrees longitude), he could find out his longitudinal position at sea.

Harrison made four of these timepieces, but he did not receive the recognition his work deserved until very late

The all-weather accuracy of the new chronometer above aided Cook in determining longitude. Its use is described in Cook's journal below.

in his life. Captain Cook was given a duplicate of Harrison's fourth chronometer, a watch-sized instrument that proved a "never-failing guide" on the second voyage.

Cook sailed from Plymouth on July 13, 1772. He was ordered to proceed this time by rounding the tip of Africa; then he was to circumnavigate the earth from west to east. If he followed instructions, he would answer at last the question of the unknown, but supposedly habitable, southern continent. He was expected to sail the seas in the highest latitudes where such a continent might be found.

Another of Cook's specific objectives was to locate a piece of land that had been seen in the South Atlantic by Jean Baptiste Bouvet, a French explorer, in 1739. Bouvet had believed his discovery might be part of the mysterious continent, so Cook made an attempt to find it. He searched in vain and eventually decided that Bouvet must have seen an iceberg and mistaken it for land. Cook had little faith in French precision, but in this case he wronged a predecessor. Bouvet's discovery was not part of a continent, but it did exist nonetheless. It is identified as Bouvet Island on modern maps, and as it is nearly two thousand miles from the nearest land, it is one of the loneliest spots in the world.

As the ships drove farther south, the temperature dropped, and Cook noted the presence of "very thick foggy weather with snow." An additional supply of rum was issued to the men, along with "fearnought" jackets made of thick cloth to keep out the cold. Soon huge islands of ice were seen, some as high as sixty feet and up to two miles around. They were a constant hazard, but their presence had one advantage. In return for the arduous labor of hacking off lumps of ice, a plentiful supply of fresh water could be obtained.

Shortly before Christmas, the outer crusts of the pack ice, which lay in vast stretches, made it necessary to swing west and then east again to find a penetrable section of ice. Cook gave Furneaux a rendezvous—Queen Charlotte Sound, New Zealand—in case the ships became separated for any reason.

On Christmas Day, according to Cook, ". . . mirth and good humor reigned throughout the whole ship." As the men of the *Resolution* had been hoarding rum from many weeks past, Cook took the precaution of shortening sail. He was aware of the hazards of plunging full speed ahead with a shipload of inebriated sailors. Of the *Adventure* he had this to say: "The crew of our consort seemed to have kept Christmas Day with the same festivity, for in the evening

Mountainous icebergs surround the Adventure *in this drawing dated January 9, 1773. Men in small boats gather chunks of ice to be melted for drinking water.*

The Adventure*'s sometimes difficult captain, Tobias Furneaux, was portrayed in 1776 by the English painter James Northcote.*

Cook selected Tahiti as one rendezvous point in the Pacific, a place for the Resolution *and the* Adventure *to meet in case they lost sight of each other. The island was also a base for American whalers in the next century, when a crewman painted this pleasant representation of Tahitian life.*

they ranged alongside of us and gave us three cheers."

By this time, Cook had sailed far beyond the temperate latitudes. But he would not break off his search. Explaining why he was compelled to go farther, he wrote, "It is a general received opinion that ice is formed near land; if so, then there must be land in the neighborhood of this ice . . ." If land lay nearby, Cook was determined to find it. The *Resolution* and the *Adventure* continued to sail southward.

Keeping within sight of each other, the two ships crossed the Antarctic Circle in mid-January, 1773. No ships before them had gone so far south. They stayed four miles apart through much of the northeasterly run, signaling to each other with gunfire whenever visibility was obscured by fog. Then on February 9, Cook reported:

The thick foggy weather continuing, and being apprehensive that the *Adventure* was still on [the starboard] tack, we . . . made the signal and tacked, to which we heard no answer. We now continued to fire a gun every half-hour . . . the fog dissipated at times so to admit us to see two or three miles or more around us; we, however, could neither hear nor see anything of her.

Cook spent the next two days in search of his consort. He gave up finally, assuming that Furneaux would pilot the *Adventure* to their New Zealand rendezvous. Before going there himself, Cook made one last penetration of the pack ice. Although the fog was now lifting, the danger persisted, as the captain recorded in his log:

. . . surrounded on every side with huge pieces of ice equally as dangerous as so many rocks, it was natural for us to wish for daylight, which, when it came, was so far from lessening the danger that it served to increase our apprehensions thereof by exhibiting to our view those mountains of ice which in the night would have passed unseen. These obstacles, together with dark nights and the advanced season of the year, discouraged me from carrying into execution a resolution I had taken of crossing the Antarctic Circle once more . . .

On March 17, certain that no further progress could be made, Cook hauled away to the northeast toward New Zealand. On the way he hoped to touch at Tasmania and try to figure out its true relation to the continent of Australia. But the wind was against him, so he abandoned the problem in the hope that Furneaux might have solved it.

Late in March, Cook made a landfall at Dusky Sound near the southwestern tip of New Zealand. Here the *Resolution* was overhauled. She had been out of sight of land for

117 days, during which wind and ice had battered her severely.

Several weeks later the *Resolution*'s sails were raised and she proceeded north along New Zealand's west coast. At daybreak on May 18 she reached Queen Charlotte Sound, where the *Adventure* had been waiting for six weeks. Furneaux came aboard the *Resolution* to report on his activities during the time the ships had been separated. He had visited Tasmania, and from his observations Cook concluded—wrongly—that this land was part of the Australian continent.

Furneaux's lack of thoroughness as an explorer was matched by his laxity as a disciplinarian, for he had not enforced the dietary rules that would prevent scurvy. As a result, one man had died aboard his ship, and twenty men lay ill with the disease. Cook himself went ashore to find wild celery and other vegetables for the men of the *Adventure*. And he impressed on Furneaux the need to feed these fresh foods to the men—along with herb juices, herb-tinctured beef broth, and preserved cabbages fermented with juniper berries. Previously, Furneaux had been loath to order his men to adhere to such a diet; now he was expected to follow Cook's good example.

While the *Resolution* lay at anchor, Cook put ashore some sheep, goats, and pigs, with which England's King George, an enthusiastic farmer, had wished to furnish the

NATIONAL MARITIME MUSEUM, GREENWICH

In navigation latitude has long been determined by measuring the angle between the sun and the horizon, as shown at right in a sixteenth-century painting of a crude sighting. The backstaff (below), invented in 1590, refined the sighting procedure. Cook's navigation benefited from an even more accurate instrument, the quadrant (left), invented around 1750.

WHITBY LITERARY AND PHILOSOPHICAL SOCIETY

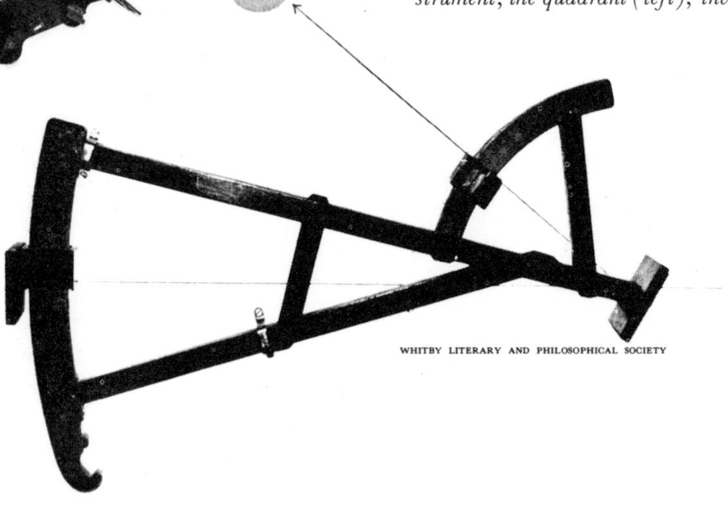

newly discovered islands. The sheep soon died after nibbling leaves from a poisonous shrub, and the Maoris killed and ate the goats. The pigs survived, however. They multiplied to such an extent that their descendants still exist in New Zealand where they are known as Captain Cookers.

With winter approaching, Furneaux had made plans for the *Adventure* to lie up in Queen Charlotte Sound. Cook entertained no such notion. He regarded the months of idleness as bad for discipline. Besides, there was a great deal of exploration that he wanted to do, and he was not prepared to wait. He hoped to traverse the entire Pacific, from New Zealand to Cape Horn, and end all doubts as to the existence of a continent extending into the temperate zones. Cook and Furneaux established two rendezvous points— one at Tahiti and one at New Zealand— in the event their ships lost sight of each other again.

The ships sailed east and south through stormy seas during June and much of July. Then on July 18, having reached longitude 133° west without seeing any land, Cook guided his vessels north toward Tahiti. Scurvy had continued to take its toll aboard the *Adventure*, and Cook was aware of the urgency of reaching some island where he might obtain more fresh vegetables. Early in the evening of August 14, the ships approached the south side of Tahiti. The incident that occurred here is described best in Cook's own words:

Two scientific members of the voyage were Johann Forster and his son Georg. The father is seen in this painting holding a bird, the son writing or drawing. Johann was unpopular with many members of the expedition, but he was a competent scientist, and he collected a great deal of original material about life in the Pacific Islands. Son Georg incurred the wrath of Cook and others when he published an account of the voyage six weeks ahead of Cook's official report.

I had given directions in what position the land was to be kept, but by some mistake it was not properly attended, for when I got up at break of day I found we were steering a wrong course and were not more than a half a league from the reef which guards the south end of the island. I immediately gave orders to haul off to the northward, and had the breeze of wind, which we now had, continued, we should have gone clear of everything, but the wind soon died away and at last flattened to a calm. We then hoisted out our boats, but even with their assistance the sloops could not be kept from nearing the reef . . .

With no wind, the ships continued to drift dangerously toward the reef, pulled by the inshore tide. As they were in shallow water, Cook did the only thing he could do: order his men to let go the anchors and hope they would hold. Luckily the *Adventure* found good holding ground at once. But the *Resolution*, more than a hundred tons heavier, rested near the bottom of the shallow water and "struck at every fall of the sea, which broke with great violence against the reef close under our stern and threatened us every moment with shipwreck . . .''

By heaving over other anchors and pulling hard on the cables, Cook's men were finally able to rescue the *Resolution* from the clutches of the tide. Propitiously, a gentle wind came up, and soon the ships were under sail once more toward the island. They anchored near shore and were surrounded at once by native canoes heaped with fruits and coconuts. Happily, Cook wrote:

The fruits we got here contributed greatly toward the recovery of the *Adventure*'s sick, many of whom were so weak when we put in as not to be able to get on deck without assistance were now so far recovered as to be able to walk about of themselves. They were put ashore under the care of the surgeon's mate every morning and taken aboard in the evening.

On August 26, late in the afternoon, the two ships reached Matavai Bay. Many of the natives who welcomed them remembered Cook from his previous expedition aboard the *Endeavour*. They crowded around him on the deck of his ship and asked about Banks and Solander, whom they remembered with unmasked fondness. Beneath the surface joy of welcoming back old friends there was a note of unrest. Internal wars had taken a toll of lives and had taxed some of the Tahitian spirit. In addition, some Spaniards had visited the island in the interval between Cook's voyages. Their purpose could not be fathomed by the Englishmen, but the impact of their visit would long be felt. The natives complained of an internal disease that had attacked and killed many islanders—an affliction they were sure the Spaniards had brought. Cook believed that although the disease had broken out on Tahiti at the time the Spaniards had come, they had not brought it with them.

On September 2, 1773, the *Resolution* and the *Adventure* left Tahiti, sailing westward to Huahine, another of the Society Islands. Despite some thieving by the natives, the two-week stay there was not unpleasant. Before leaving, an islander named Omai was taken aboard the *Adventure*. Furneaux wanted to take him home to England so that interested men like Banks could observe how a member of a primitive culture behaved. Omai became the first South Sea Islander to visit England and return safely to his home.

Cook's ships sailed next to the Tonga Islands group. The people here were so hospitable, and the landscape was so beautiful, that Cook renamed this group the Friendly

TEXT CONTINUED ON PAGE 88

Among the Forster drawings made on the voyage were those of a king-fisher, top, and a penguin, beneath.

85

The Resolution, *far left, with the* Adventure *beside her, rests in a sun-filled Tahitian bay between her antarctic trips. This oil painting was done by William Hodges, a landscape artist who was on Cook's second expedition.*

TEXT CONTINUED FROM PAGE 85

Islands. Then on October 7 he set sail for New Zealand.

Navigation was hampered by heavy squalls and became almost impossible when a northwest gale blew up. The *Resolution* adhered to her course despite the cruel winds, but she soon lost sight of the *Adventure*. Cook piloted his ship to his old anchorage in Queen Charlotte Sound and waited. One week passed, then two and three; there was no sign of the *Adventure*. Cook became impatient, for it was already late November. If he allowed much more time to pass, the southern summer would be over before he could cross the Pacific again as he planned. He left Furneaux a message sealed in a bottle. He buried the bottle beside the stump of a tree on which he carved, "Look underneath." Then he sailed southwest into the unmapped latitudes of the South Pacific.

Ice had completely surrounded his ship by the time he reached latitude 66° south. When fog too enveloped the ship, Cook guided her northward until there was a break

"Wood and water is easily to be had," wrote Furneaux about Tolago Bay, a New Zealand inlet Cook's ships visited several times. The picture at left is a pen drawing of the bay made by Cook. At right is a photograph of another site on the North Island of New Zealand where Cook's crew found fresh water—the Bay of Islands.

in the weather. Turning southward she again crossed the Antarctic Circle, exceeding the southernmost limit of the previous season's voyage. Now the ship's frozen sails were as stiff as metal sheets, and the men on deck were encrusted with snow, as though wearing white armor. The temperature hovered at zero as the *Resolution* drifted slowly northward once more through the masses of pack ice.

Christmas Day, 1773, found the men of the *Resolution* far less exuberant than they had been a year before. They were healthy; there was not a trace of scurvy, and only a few of them had been felled by exposure to the weather. But it was hard to be cheerful, for in the freezing waters around the ship, sixty icebergs could be seen. Wrote the botanist Johann Forster, "The whole scene looks like the wreck of a shattered world."

A month later the *Resolution* crossed the Antarctic Circle again, this time attaining latitude 71° 10'—more than four degrees inside the circle. This was farther south than Cook or anyone else had ever sailed. The achievement was duly recorded in the ship's log, but it brought no elation, only this comment from Cook:

. . . I should not have hesitated one moment in declaring it as my opinion that the ice we now see extended in a solid body quite to the pole and that it is here (i.e., to the south of this parallel) where the many ice islands we find floating about in the sea are first formed and afterwards broke off by gales of wind and other causes . . . I will not say it was impossible anywhere to get in among this ice, but I will assert that the bare attempting of it would be a very dangerous enterprise and what I believe no man in my situation would have thought of.

Cook would sail no farther in the South Pacific to look for the mysterious continent. If a solid body of ice was what

On Easter Island Cook noted huge stone statues whose origins remain uncertain to this day. Below, the French explorer La Pérouse is seen measuring one of the statues while languorous natives watch him.

FERRARIO, *Il Costume Antico e Moderno*, 18

90

geographers were looking for, as far as Cook was concerned they were welcome to it. No European could ever hope to settle in such desolation.

Cook had no choice but to turn north now. His original instructions had ordered him to circumnavigate the globe and return home by way of the Cape of Good Hope. He was not yet ready for the homeward voyage. As he recorded in his journal, he was reluctant to leave the Pacific, ". . . for although I had proved there was no continent, there remained, nevertheless, room for very large islands . . . and many of those which were formerly discovered are but imperfectly explored . . ."

The first landfall of the northern retreat was Easter Island, which had been discovered by the Dutchman Jacob Roggeveen in 1722. Cook anchored the *Resolution* and rowed ashore, eager to confirm Roggeveen's observation that the island was green and richly fertile. Unhappily, he found that in the fifty-two years since the Dutchman's visit, a change had taken place. Or perhaps Roggeveen had been mistaken. The land was now parched and dry. Gone was the lush foliage, and the once-tall trees were now no taller than ten feet. Cook wrote:

The Easter Island statues still stand, fifteen to thirty feet high (compare with man's height); but their topknots have been knocked off.

No nation will ever contend for the honor of the discovery of Easter Island, as there is hardly an island in this sea which affords less refreshments and convenience for shipping than it does. Nature has hardly provided it with anything fit for man to eat or drink, and as the natives are but few and may be supposed to plant no more than sufficient for themselves, they cannot have much to spare to newcomers.

Cook found the natives friendly, however. Their language as well as their temperament was akin to that of the Tahitians. They were not averse to trade, he reported, so he was able to exchange some medals "and other trifles" for potatoes, plantains, and sugar cane. These foodstuffs provided a welcome change from the usual ship's fare. Cook noted that the enormous stone statues on Easter Island were not worshiped openly by the natives as the Dutch said they had been. Perhaps these great carved figures were now only burial markers for tribes or native families; he could not say for certain.

Cook sailed on. After a brief stay in the Marquesas Islands, which the Spanish explorer Alvaro de Mendaña had discovered in 1595, the *Resolution* reached Tahiti once again late in April 1774. For the Englishmen this visit was made memorable by the appearance of an armada of native

Omai, the adventurous islander who joined the expedition, was painted by Sir Joshua Reynolds. In the drawing at right, from an early edition of Cook's journal, Omai's boat is sailing close to shore, where natives are gathering. Cook's two ships lie out in the harbor.

double canoes. There were more than three hundred boats carrying fifteen hundred warriors in full war dress. Cook learned that the fleet had been organized to assault Mooréa, a nearby island that was at war with some of the Tahitian chiefs. Much as he wished to, Cook did not remain long in Tahiti. He was aware that the natives wanted their English visitors gone before the great battle began.

In July, after sailing westward, Cook arrived in an island group that he called the New Hebrides. Here the people were black, rather fuzzy-haired, and as Cook was soon to learn, fierce. He recorded graphically what happened when he and two boatloads of men rowed from the *Resolution* toward a beach on one of the islands:

Several people appeared on the shore and by signs invited us to go to them. . . When they saw I was determined to proceed to some other place, they ran along the shore, keeping always abreast of the boats, and at last directed us to a place, a sandy beach, where I could step out of the boat without wetting a foot.

I landed in the face of a great multitude with nothing but a green branch in my hand [which] I had got from one of them. I was received very courteously, and upon their pressing near the boat, retired upon my making signs to keep off. One man who seemed to be a chief . . . made them form a kind of semicircle round the bow of the boat and beat anyone who broke through this order . . . I was charmed with their behavior; the only thing which could give the least suspicion was the most of them being armed with clubs, darts, stones, and bows and arrows.

Cook reported that the chief then made a sign for him to haul the boat up on shore. Desiring instead to return to the *Resolution*, Cook stepped back into his boat—but the natives seized his oars. Pointing his musket did not stop them from pulling the boat onto the beach. Cook wrote:

RICKMAN, *Journal of Captain Cook*, 1781

*Cook probably saw masks like this
in the New Hebrides islands where
they were worn in dramatic rituals.*

Our own safety became now the only consideration, and yet I was very loath to fire upon such a multitude and resolved to make the chief alone fall a victim to his own treachery. But my musket at this critical moment refused to perform its part and made it absolutely necessary for me to give orders to fire, as they now began to shoot their arrows and throw darts and stones at us. The first discharge threw them into confusion, but another discharge was hardly sufficient to drive them off the beach, and after all they continued to throw stones from behind the trees and bushes, and one would peep out now and then and throw a dart. . .

Friendship with these natives was obviously out of the question, so the *Resolution* sailed immediately for Tana, the southernmost island in the group. Here the natives seemed more hospitable. They welcomed their visitors with gifts of coconuts but eventually proved no less disagreeable than their brethren on the neighboring island.

Cook sailed now to his New Zealand base and anchored in Queen Charlotte Sound on October 18, 1774. He learned from the Maoris that the *Adventure* had been there and gone; the sight of stumps where trees had once stood substantiated this. Cook was unable to learn what had happened to either the ship or her men. The bottle that contained his message to Furneaux had been removed from its site, but no message for the captain had been buried in its place.

Cook was not to know until much later that Furneaux and the *Adventure* had reached the rendezvous more than ten months earlier on December 1, 1773. This was just six days after Cook had left New Zealand to cross the Antarctic Circle. Furneaux remained in Queen Charlotte Sound almost a month, but his stay had not ended pleasantly. When he was ready to leave, he sent a party of eleven men ashore to gather vegetables. A day passed and the men did not return, so Furneaux sent out another party to investigate. On the beach where the first party had landed, the searchers found all the signs of a cannibal feast. There were baskets full of roasted meat—"Such a shocking scene of carnage and barbarity as can never be mentioned but with horror," said one of the men. Thus the fate of the missing seamen had been determined.

Furneaux gave the order to weigh anchor as soon as his search party returned. Steering homeward, he passed four hundred miles south of Cape Horn and then crossed the South Atlantic. Here he scoured the high latitudes, searching vainly for Bouvet Island. Finding nothing, he set a

This mask, believed to represent a water spirit, comes from New Caledonia, south of the New Hebrides.

course for Cape Town, South Africa, where his ship was refitted for the last leg of her journey. She reached Portsmouth, England, on July 14, 1774. Arriving home a full year before Cook, Furneaux became the first English commander to circumnavigate the globe from west to east.

Furneaux was still recounting his exploits in the South Pacific when James Cook reached Cape Horn in late December, 1774, forty-one days after leaving New Zealand. His mission was almost completed. He had swept the South Pacific, and though he had devoted much of his voyage to a

vain search, he had in fact achieved his primary object. For he wrote, "If I have failed in discovering a continent, it is because it does not exist in a navigable sea . . ." With icy recollections of the weeks spent in frozen waters, Cook did not envy anyone who might attempt to follow in his tracks.

The *Resolution*'s third Christmas was spent in a miserable cove on the shores of Tierra del Fuego. Cook still had some bottles of Madeira. With these and "goose pie" made with local sea birds, he and his men were able to spend the

One of the most impressive spectacles that Cook and his men saw in the Pacific, just before they left Tahiti, was this scene painted by Hodges—Tahitian war canoes setting out for a great naval battle.

holiday cheerfully. They rejoiced at the thought that with luck their next Christmas would be celebrated at home.

Early in January, 1775, Cook sailed into the Atlantic and took possession of South Georgia and an island group he later named after the Earl of Sandwich. Then he made one last sweep of the empty sea on the chance of finding a continent in the South Atlantic. He also hoped to spot Bouvet's alleged discovery, the search for which had begun his second voyage. A glance at Cook's homeward route (see end sheets) reveals that the explorer passed within one degree latitude of Bouvet Island. He may even have been near enough to see it, but thinking it was an island of ice, continued toward the tip of South Africa.

Before reaching Table Bay, Cook fell in with a Dutch cargo vessel of the East India Company. Her captain gave Cook some sorely needed supplies and told him of Furneaux's arrival in England some months before. At Cape Town, the *Resolution* underwent a month-long refitting. Her rigging had been damaged severely; she was in good shape otherwise, which was astounding, considering that she had sailed over fifty thousand miles.

Late in April the voyage was resumed. The *Resolution*, heading north in the Atlantic, called at the islands of St. Helena and Ascension, and finally the Azores. On July 29, 1775, land was seen near Plymouth. A day later the ship anchored at Portsmouth, and Cook and some of the civilian members of the expedition took a coach to London. Their ocean voyage had lasted three years and eighteen days, the longest of its kind in history. And to add to its astonishing record of performance, only four deaths had occurred on Cook's ship—three by accident and one from disease, none from scurvy.

On two far-reaching surveys of the Pacific, Cook had discovered a host of new islands and had made a chart of the Central and South Pacific that was unprecedented in its accuracy. He had waged a totally effective war against scurvy, and by using Harrison's chronometer, had proved how longitude might be simply and accurately determined. The fabled southern continent was still unknown, but Cook had proved that if the continent existed, it could be found only in a desperately cold area. Thus Dalrymple's theory of a temperate continent had finally been shattered.

In summing up the results of his exploration, Cook stated, "I can be bold enough to say that no man will ever venture farther than I have done; and that the lands which may be to the south will never be explored."

The Resolution *ventured once more into unknown and icy seas, the South Atlantic, before heading at last for England.*

POLYNESIAN ADVENTURERS

James Cook's return to England was trumpeted throughout the land. The English people and their king gave him a stirring reception that befitted a man who had made the greatest ocean voyage in history. He was given the rank of post captain, and as an added honor he was appointed a captain of the Royal Hospital for Seamen at Greenwich. The Royal Society elected him a fellow and eventually accorded him its highest award, the Copley Gold Medal. He was invited to sit for the artist Nathaniel Dance, whose painting (see cover) portrayed Cook as a man of great natural dignity and was considered an excellent likeness by his friends and fellow voyagers.

Cook was not the only man to be acclaimed after the second voyage. Omai, the Society Islander who had been brought to England aboard the *Adventure*, was also a great success. London society and people of every rank were charmed by him. And he was delighted by everyone he met —including the English monarch, of whom he said, "King Tosh, very good man."

Omai was transformed considerably during his stay in England. He developed an urbane manner and wore fine clothes made especially for him. In sharp contrast to the nobleman's façade was the Polynesian's brown skin, long hair, and blazing dark eyes. Londoners thought him an amusing oddity, and they enjoyed his wit and disarming naïveté. Moreover, they marveled at how much he seemed to know about the history of his island home, the islands nearby, and the whole South Sea Island civilization as well.

Cook knew that Omai was not uniquely well informed in this respect. On his first visit among the Society Islanders the explorer had noted that "these people have an extensive knowledge of the islands situated in these seas . . ." And on his third voyage, recognizing that Hawaiians were of the same race as Tahitians, the explorer was to write:

How shall we account for this nation spreading itself so far over

In the foreground of this Hodges painting are two native boats of Tahiti: a small double canoe used by chieftains, and a single canoe with an outrigger.

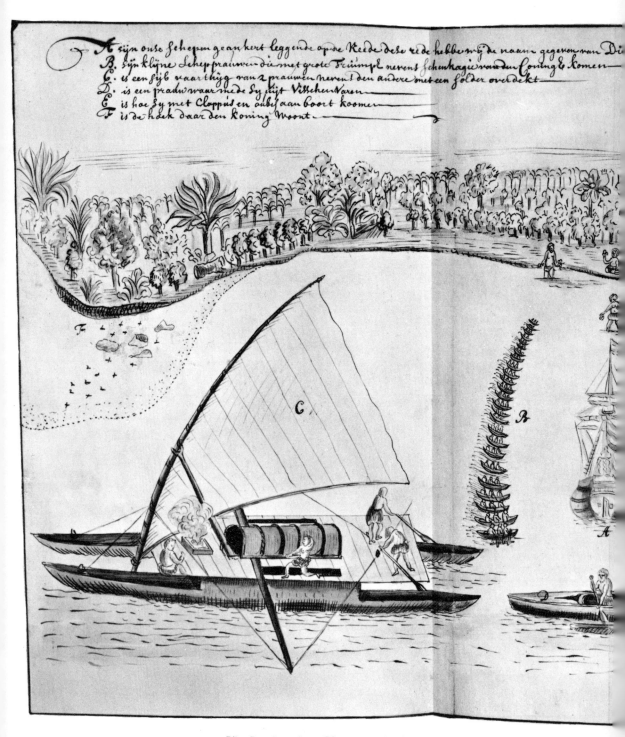

The Dutch explorer Tasman made this pen-and-ink sketch in 1643 on a visit to Tongatabu in the Friendly Islands. His ships are at right, anchored near a long line of native canoes. A large double canoe is at left. On the platform that joins its twin hulls, a fire burns—to cook food on long voyages. The two men at the stern use steering paddles to guide the canoe.

this vast ocean? We find them from New Zealand to the south, to [Hawaii] to the north, and from Easter Island to the Hebrides. . . . How much farther is not known, but we may safely conclude that they extend to the west beyond the Hebrides.

Generations of explorers who followed Cook were similarly puzzled. None of them were able to account for the native migration; they only confirmed the fact that the South Sea Islanders had traveled widely and learned much throughout their history. Indeed, long before Balboa first saw the mighty Pacific, native adventurers in canoes crafted from gouged-out tree trunks were sailing the ocean's breadth and colonizing its myriad islands.

The movement of this primitive people was gradual. Hundreds of years were required to populate as many islands as James Cook visited on one three-year voyage. The early travelers were not blessed with Cook's knowledge of geography. Nor did they possess such refinements of navigation as the compass, the sextant, or the backstaff—or even primitive versions thereof. They guided their canoes by the sun and the stars, the wind, and their awareness of the shifting ocean currents. Long before men like Columbus and Magellan dared to sail beyond sight of land, the ancestors of the South Sea Islanders were settling on distant shores. These people have come to be recognized as perhaps the most skilled navigators, the most courageous sailors, of the ancient world.

Many anthropologists have agreed that the first Pacific voyagers came from various parts of Asia. These Stone Age peoples were probably pushed from their mainland homes by the arrival of other—doubtless stronger—races. Or perhaps they were compelled by famine to seek new homelands in order to find food.

They migrated east and later south, along the Malay Peninsula. From there it was a relatively short distance to Indonesia, the island group that includes Sumatra, Java, Borneo, and the Moluccas. Living close to the sea, these former landsmen had to change their way of life. Over the course of many generations they learned to fish, build boats, and sail. And when they emigrated again, for whatever reasons, they moved even farther away—to New Guinea, Australia, Tasmania. The distances seemed great, but the bays and straits were so dotted with islands that land was seldom far out of sight.

Sometime during the last few centuries before Christianity, the islands in the western Pacific were finally settled. But several hundred years passed before the unin-

habited islands of the central Pacific were colonized. This region came to be called Polynesia (a word whose Greek roots mean "many islands"). Shaped like the head of a spear pointing east, Polynesia extends from New Zealand in the south to Hawaii in the north, and to the apex of the triangle, Easter Island. (See map on page 112.)

Settlement of Polynesia, or the Polynesian triangle, is believed to have begun in the fifth century. How the first inhabitants reached this region has been debated for much of the time since then. Early theorists maintained that the Polynesian voyagers traveled southeast through Melanesia (meaning roughly, "islands of dark-skinned people"), which includes the Solomon Islands, the New Hebrides, and the Fiji Islands.

This theory was later rejected by scientists who observed some basic physical differences between the Polynesians and the Melanesians. The inhabitants of Melanesia are predominantly woolly-haired, with dark skin like the aborigines of Australia. The Polynesians are paler; their hair tends to be straight and their features more Caucasian. Despite some variations, the language of the Pacific Islanders is similar throughout both regions. Thus, some scientists suspect the Polynesians did migrate to Melanesia—but only after the great triangle itself had first been peopled.

The only other possible route from west to east lay north of Melanesia. It passed through an island chain called Micronesia ("little islands"), which includes the Caroline, Marshall, and Gilbert islands. The Micronesian route is considered the most likely, but the precise path the natives followed may never be discovered. All that is known for certain is that they must have reached the central Pacific by traveling from island to island in a gradual migration.

Another mystery that may never be solved concerns the motive behind the push to the central Pacific. Did the Polynesians' ancestors fill their canoes with livestock and foodstuffs and set out deliberately to find new places to live? Or did their colonizing result from shipwrecks and the accident of boats being blown off course and running aground

The natives on these pages are all Pacific Islanders, and they may possibly have a common ancestry. Yet, aside from their unruly hair, they could hardly look less alike. The Australian aborigine (top) is very dark and belongs to an isolated culture; the swarthy Hawaiian warrior (above) and the light-skinned Tahitian (right) are members of the expansive Polynesian culture.

on foreign shores? Cook came to favor the latter argument because of a personal experience.

When he reached Atiu on his third voyage, four Tahitians were found living on the island. Omai, who was still traveling with Cook, was astonished, for Atiu was six hundred miles from Tahiti. Omai learned that some time earlier the four natives had been sailing in a canoe bound for Raiatea, about a hundred miles west of Tahiti. A violent gale had blown them off course, and rough seas had capsized their boat. Only four of the twenty persons aboard had survived the voyage. Starved and terrified, they had clung to the overturned craft for many days until some natives on Atiu had seen it on the surf and brought it ashore.

Fascinated by the story, which Omai related to him, Captain Cook wrote in his journal, "This circumstance very well accounts for the manner the inhabited islands in the sea have been at first peopled; especially those which lay remote from any continent and from each other."

Whether or not he was correct, an entire civilization did migrate gradually across the Pacific. Only the means of transportation by which this migration was accomplished is known for certain. The people became excellent navigators and learned to build seaworthy boats. Their shipbuilding skills were so proficient, in fact, that Cook was prompted to write:

When one considers the tools these people have to work with, one cannot help but admire their workmanship; these are adzes and small hatchets made of hard stone, chisels or gouges made of human bones—generally the bones of the forearm—but spike nails [from visiting ships] have pretty well supplied the place of these. With these ordinary tools that a European workman would expect to break [on] the first stroke, I have seen them work surprisingly fast.

Each Polynesian shipwright had his own set of tools. Each tool was shaped differently for its own particular use and attached to a wooden handle with coconut fiber or sennit braid. The natives worked deftly, shaping the trunks of felled trees into long strips which when joined became smooth, seaworthy hulls. When the adzes became dull from constant use, they were sharpened on sandstone blocks. And when friction made them hot and brittle, they were sunk briefly into the cool, juicy trunks of banana trees.

In many parts of the Pacific, the god of the forest was Tane, to whom the natives prayed before putting their adzes to a tree. By this ritual the god was asked to consent to the

Drawings made on Bougainville's expedition compare two outrigger canoes. The hull of the top one is round-bottomed; the other is wedge-shaped with a high, curved stern.

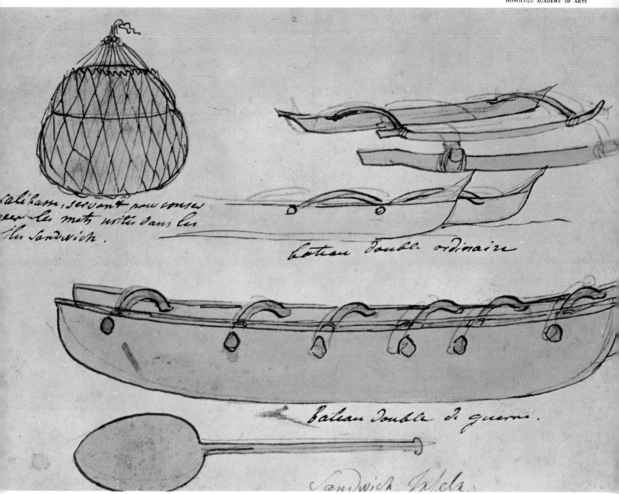

ale'bass, servant pow conses eev les mets utter dans les illes Sandwich.

boteau Double ordinaire

bateau Double de guerre.

Sandwich Islds.

The Russian artist Louis Choris, who went around the world in 1816, drew these examples of wood crafts-manship in Hawaii: a food jar (top left), pieces of outrigger yokes (top right), a paddle (bottom), and a pair of Hawaiian double canoes.

taking of a tree. The canoe that was then made was dedicated to Tane, and an altar to him was built on the boat. The natives made daily offerings so that the god's wrath would not fall on those who sailed the boat.

The size of a canoe usually corresponded to the type of voyage on which it would be used. Larger boats were generally sixty or eighty feet long, but some are known to have reached a hundred feet. These could carry sixty people, along with their pigs and dogs and a supply of fresh vegetables—or a hundred warriors, fully armed.

Slim, tapered, and expertly shaped to glide through the water, the native canoes could often reach twenty knots—a speed that astonished European sailors, whose ships normally traveled much slower. Long paddles were used as rudders to steer the canoes. Smaller paddles helped propel

TEXT CONTINUED ON PAGE 110

A SEAWORTHY CANOE

Louis Choris filled his sketchbooks with impressions during his global voyage. Here are drawings of a canoe he saw on one of the Marshall Islands. The outrigger attachment can be seen best in the detailed front and top views (far right). The side view (below) shows the rigging. For a long time, explorers had wanted to know how the sails of a native canoe were handled. It was Cook who reported that although the craft could travel "with either end foremost," its sails could be tacked whenever the wind changed. Choris' drawings complement the descriptions in Cook's journals. Cook wrote that the Polynesian canoe was "about twenty-four feet long, and the bottom for the most part formed in one piece . . . The sides consist of three boards . . . neatly fitted and lashed to the bottom part. The extremities of both head and stern [are] a little raised, and both are made sharp . . ." The crew and passengers who sailed on canoes of this design sat on the platform that extended from hull to outrigger.

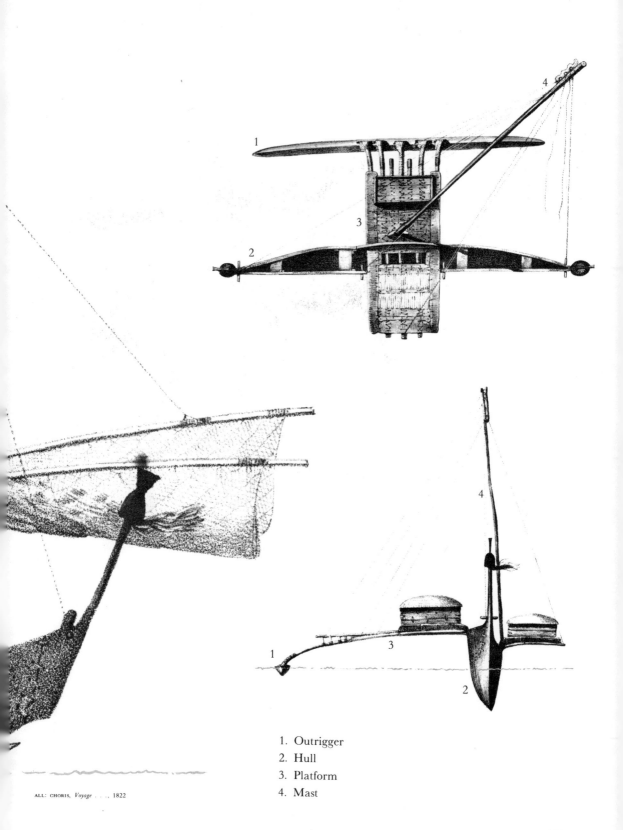

1. Outrigger
2. Hull
3. Platform
4. Mast

Choris transformed his impressions of the South Seas into a series of handsome water-color paintings. In this one, Hawaiian warriors perform before a royal court. They carry feathery shields which they shake and twirl as they dance.

TEXT CONTINUED FROM PAGE 107

them, as did the wind that filled their sails. These sails were pieced together from a cloth made of the dried, swordlike leaves of pandanus trees.

Many canoes were provided with an outrigger, which extended to the side to help balance the narrow boats and prevent them from capsizing. However, each of the larger canoes, built to carry supplies and people on long voyages, had a second canoe joined to it in place of the outrigger. Boats built this way were called double canoes.

On these double canoes, some of which had as many as three wooden masts, the Polynesians' ancestors took their language, customs, culture, and traditions to the farthest

110

Pacific Islands. And the plants and animals that were carried with them provided food for the generations that succeeded them in the new lands.

The pigs, dogs, and fowl that are found in Polynesia today came from the southeastern portion of the Asian continent. So did breadfruit, bananas, plantains, and coconuts. The sweet potato had a surprisingly different story. Its origin has been traced not to Asia but South America. Men believed at first that early Spanish explorers had brought this vegetable to the Pacific; but later, scientists determined that the sweet potato had come to Polynesia even before Columbus discovered America. One explanation is that a

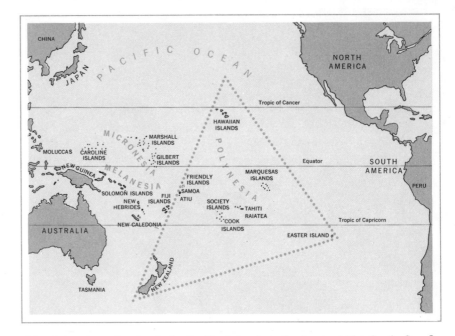

The Polynesian triangle of the Pacific (above) is the heart of the South Sea Island civilization. Yet it has always been a source of mystery, for no one knows where the Polynesians' ancestors came from. The only certainty is that they migrated by sailing in large canoes like those shown in the Hodges drawing below.

host of South American Indians, set adrift in the Pacific on crudely fashioned rafts, were swept along by the ocean currents and southeasterly trade winds to an island in central Polynesia. The possibility that such a voyage could have occurred was confirmed in 1947 by a Norwegian explorer, Thor Heyerdahl. Aboard a raft he called the *Kon-Tiki*, Heyerdahl drifted from the west coast of Peru to the heart of the South Pacific. He covered 4,300 miles in 101 days.

Heyerdahl's achievement is unquestioned, but his theory of emigration has not been proved. A more widely accepted explanation for the presence of sweet potatoes in the Pacific is that a native expedition (perhaps only one canoe) sailed from Polynesia to Peru—for what purpose no one knows—and then returned to its homeland.

This expedition must have embarked some five hundred years before Omai left home on the *Adventure*. The voyage would have been long and hard, bucking the southeasterly trade winds. But with a push from an occasional westerly wind, the travelers could have completed the trip in three weeks. Perhaps they were not so fortunate. Perhaps their food and water supply began to run low and they had to ration themselves to make their stores last as long as possible. And they might have thought they were doomed —until finally a bird flew overhead one day. Then they probably saw twigs floating in the water, and patches of seaweed as well. These were signs the Polynesian navigators had come to recognize, and no doubt they cried aloud with joy and relief.

Soon land appeared. It was an awesome sight, a line of mountains that stretched as far as the horizon. The travelers sailed onward, eagerly propelling their boats toward the shore. What they discovered was not a friendly land. The terrain was forbidding, and the natives they encountered were hostile. The Polynesians probably did not stay long because they feared they might never get back. But with the trade winds at their backs, navigation was relatively simple, and the voyagers succeeded in finding their way home. They brought tales of the long, weary days at sea and of the strange, frightening land they had seen. They also carried tangible, permanent evidence of their transoceanic achievement: the mellow sweet potato.

Although the names of these courageous travelers are unknown, they were the first heroes of exploration in the Pacific. They crossed the mighty ocean and found its eastern limits, and they returned home to tell of it.

To aid navigation, the South Sea Islanders fashioned crude charts from dried sticks. Cowry shells were sewn on to locate the islands.

THE CULT OF THE "NOBLE SAVAGE"

From explorers' tales, Europe came to know of the blissful life of the South Sea Islanders, at peace with the world and in harmony with nature. Such stories had a special appeal for upper-class Europeans of the eighteenth century. Theirs was an age of powdered wigs and frills, elegance and courtly manners. As they were accustomed to city life and to the rigidity of a social scale, they yearned for the freedom that seemed to be enjoyed only by primitive peoples. The Polynesians were envied above all. Those who studied such wild cultures became members of a cult in which the native was not looked upon as a simple primitive, but as a "noble savage." Artists with similar feelings encouraged the cult: men like Cook's artist William Hodges, whose works romanticized and strangely altered the natives. The Hodges scene below shows Cook landing at the Friendly Islands. He is greeted by natives draped in the flowing costumes of ancient Romans or Greeks. Somewhat more realistic is the sketch above of native dancers made in 1793 by the French explorer Bruni d'Entrecasteaux. Perhaps the most decorative expression of the sentiments of the "noble savage" cult was a wallpaper design in several panels, one of which is at left. This panel shows carefully posed native musicians

TEXT CONTINUED ON PAGE 117

115

TEXT CONTINUED FROM PAGE 115

in lush, yet unrealistic surroundings. Created in France in 1804–5, the entire design represented each place Cook had visited. Painters, however, were not alone in glorifying the South Pacific. In *Robinson Crusoe*, written in 1719, the English novelist Daniel Defoe popularized the simplicity of life on a desolate island. His work was followed some years later by that of the French philosopher Jean Jacques Rousseau, who made the strongest contributions to further the cult. Rousseau's writings reflect his love for the beauty of nature and his disdain of civilization. He believed the primitive life was the better life because it was close to nature. Rousseau was a man who experienced great joy just walking in the country, a man who wrote, "I feel ecstasies, ineffable delights . . . in identifying myself with the whole of nature." Because of Rousseau and

others, the lure of the tropics worked its magic on later Europeans as well. Among them was Scotland's Robert Louis Stevenson, who spent the last years of his life in Samoa. Here he wrote stories and articles for European publishers and was known to the natives as the "teller of tales." Stevenson's Pacific tales reveal a preference for the purity of thought and action attributed to the Polynesians. So do the works of Paul Gauguin, who gave up the French business world in 1890 for an artist's life in Tahiti. His paintings reflect the simple beauty of Polynesia in brilliant hues that are suggestive of drenching sunlight. Gauguin helped further the myth of the "noble savage" not by romanticizing the life he saw, but by showing it honestly and in all its true richness. At left is Gauguin's *Street in Tahiti*, which captures the timeless appeal of the Polynesians' existence.

Robert Louis Stevenson
(1850–1894)

Jean Jacques Rousseau
(1712–1778)

Daniel Defoe
(1659–1731)

117

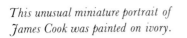
*This unusual miniature portrait of
James Cook was painted on ivory.*

VI

A NORTHERN PASSAGE

Captain Cook remained bound to his desk for several months after completing his second voyage. He finished editing his journal, and he attended to some of the duties required of his position at the Royal Hospital. He spent time at home with his wife and two of their sons, but he grew restless. He had been highly honored; now the joy of returning home safely to England was wearing off. In a note to his old friend John Walker, he wrote:

My fate drives me from one extreme to another; a few months ago the whole Southern Hemisphere was hardly big enough for me, and now I am going to be confined to the limits of Greenwich Hospital, which are far too small for an active mind like mine. I must confess it is a fine retreat and pretty income, but whether I can bring myself to like ease and retirement, time will show.

He made little attempt to learn to like his new life. He was forty-seven, not too old for yet one more voyage, so his impatience to get underway again can be understood. And he soon got his wish. In February, 1776, at a dinner in the home of the Earl of Sandwich, who was First Lord of the Admiralty, the final chapter of Cook's career at sea began.

The topic of conversation that evening was England's renewed interest in finding a northern sea route from the Atlantic Ocean to the Pacific. If such a route existed, it would be a boon to trade, for it would certainly be shorter than the course around the Cape of Good Hope and probably less dangerous than the route around Cape Horn. England had been seeking this passage sporadically, and unsuccessfully, for two hundred years. Her interest had quickened once again early in the eighteenth century when Vitus Bering, a Danish navigator in the service of Russia, had discovered the channel (now called Bering Strait) that separates the Asian and North American continents.

The English were so certain that this strait led to a pas-

AMERICAN MUSEUM OF NATURAL HISTORY

The art of carving totem poles was highly developed by the Haida Indians of North America. Cook believed Indians were a mysterious, unkempt, but not uncultured people.

Numbers superimposed on this map of the third voyage indicate important stops: 1. King George's Sound (now called Nootka Sound); 2. Sandwich Sound (Prince William Sound); 3. Hinchinbrook Sound (Cook Inlet—leading to Anchorage); 4. Cook's "farthest north"; and 5. the Aleutian Islands, appearing too close to Asia.

sage over the top of the world that Parliament voted a prize of twenty thousand pounds to the first man who found that passage. Cook felt it was his duty as well as his destiny to undertake the search, and when the Admiralty offered him command of an expedition, the offer was immediately accepted. Exuberantly he wrote Walker: "I have quitted an easy retirement for an active, perhaps dangerous voyage. I embark on as fair a prospect as I can wish."

Cook's judgment of the nature of the voyage was correct, but he made a serious misjudgment when he chose to sail in the *Resolution* again. Although the ship had survived the extremes of tropical heat and Antarctic cold in the southern seas, she was not in good sailing condition, and she proved a liability. Cook's consort ship, the *Discovery* (another Whitby collier), was much smaller than the *Resolution*, but she outperformed the mother ship.

Command of the *Discovery* was given to Charles Clerke, who had sailed with Cook twice before. Cook's first lieutenant on the *Resolution* was John Gore, already one of the most experienced officers in the navy. He had been around the world with Wallis and had accompanied Cook on the first South Sea voyage.

Other members of the expedition included George Vancouver, a young midshipman who would later lead an expedition to the Pacific and make important discoveries along the North American coast; William Bligh, sailing master on the *Resolution*, whose crew would stage a mutiny

TEXT CONTINUED ON PAGE 124

BOTH: NATIONAL PORTRAIT GALLERY, LONDON

The portraits of these two portly gentlemen show them several years after they sailed with Cook. Both William Bligh (above) and George Vancouver eventually gained fame as captains of their own vessels.

Cook hoped that inlets like Nootka Sound (above) would lead over the top of North America. This water col

surgeon's mate *William Ellis shows the tents that scientists of the expedition pitched on a rocky promontory.*

TEXT CONTINUED FROM PAGE 121

against his command of the *Bounty* thirteen years hence; and Omai, who was now to be returned to his homeland.

William Bayly, the astronomer aboard the *Adventure*, made plans to sail again, but the artist William Hodges did not. His place was taken by a Swiss painter named John Webber.

The ships carried a large supply of vegetable seeds and some livestock that were to be presented, as gifts from King George, to the people of the Pacific Islands. There was a bull, two cows with their calves, and some pedigreed sheep. Cook remarked that the *Resolution* was like Noah's Ark, ". . . lacking only a few females of our own species."

On July 12, 1776, the day before the fourth anniversary of the start of his second voyage, James Cook set sail from Plymouth. Both ships did not leave England at the same time. Clerke was detained because of his involvement in the financial woes of a close friend, so the *Resolution* sailed ahead of the *Discovery*. The captains planned a rendezvous at Table Bay, at the tip of South Africa, the last civilized place Cook would touch for a long time.

The voyage south to the Cape of Good Hope proved that Cook's ship was in no condition for the undertaking he had planned. But he would not turn back. He was forced to put up with the bad calking and bothersome leaks. Some repairs were made as he awaited the arrival of the *Discovery*. At the end of November he and Clerke sailed southeastward together, according to their instructions.

Their course would take them across the Indian Ocean; then, once in the Pacific, they would head north and carefully examine the North American and Asian coasts in the hope of finding a channel leading either to the east or the west.

Christmas, 1776, was spent in the South Indian Ocean. The ships were anchored off a lonely spot that was eventually named Kerguélen Island after its discoverer, Yves Joseph de Kerguélen. Here the crews were happy to eat birds and seal meat, instead of the usual ship's fare.

Continuing eastward, Cook's ships become enveloped in fog. Then a squall came up, and the *Resolution*'s masts were so damaged they could not be wholly repaired until the expedition reached Tasmania late in January. Cook found the Tasmanians a simple people whose houses were like huge birds' nests made of sticks and tree bark. The people lived on the coast but had no knowledge of fishing; they were content to scoop up mussels and other shellfish from the shallow inshore waters.

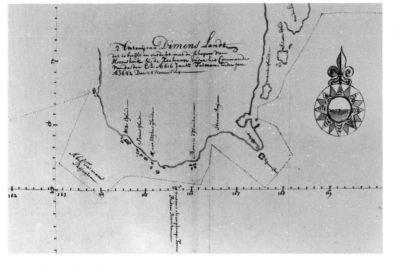

FERRARIO, *Il Costume Antico e Moderno*, 1815

The southern coast of Tasmania (Van Diemen's Land on the map at left) was charted by Tasman in 1642. Little was known about the original Tasmanians, shown below with their bark canoes, until Cook visited the island in 1777 and described the natives in his journal.

125

Although Cook had not been on the island before, he did not remain there long enough to survey it. If he had done so, he might have altered his notion that Tasmania was connected to the Australian mainland.

Early in February the ships sailed on. Cook was eager to reach New Zealand and, if possible, learn why crew members of Furneaux's *Adventure* had been murdered during a stop-off on the second voyage. He entered the familiar anchorage at Queen Charlotte Sound on February 12, 1777, and began making inquiries. Few natives would board his ship at first. They were sure Cook had come back just for revenge. He finally pried the story of the massacre from some of the Maoris who remembered him, but he did not seek retaliation. He could not be certain of the exact circumstances of the bloody incident, nor could he determine which side had been responsible for starting it. In not responding with violence, Cook probably acted justly, but it was never easy for a man of his choleric temperament to strike a proper balance between severity and leniency.

Sailing from New Zealand on a northeasterly course, Cook stopped at an island group that now bears his name. Then he swung west again to the Friendly Islands. The natives there treated him hospitably, but thievery continued to be a problem. Omai could not convince the people not to steal, nor was the threat of killing captured thieves an effective deterrent. However, Cook devised a means for recovering stolen articles: native chieftains or other important men of a tribe were held as hostages until the missing items were brought back. This nearly always proved successful.

Because of contrary winds, Cook could not make for Tahiti when he wanted to, so he remained for a time in the Friendly Islands, which he found to his liking. When spring came, Cook sailed forth and landed the animals from his "Noah's Ark" at Tahiti. He also deposited Omai, who in little more than three years had seen more of the world than any Polynesian before him. Omai astonished his friends with his Western manners and extravagant behavior. He strutted about in European clothes, firing his pistols in the air and rashly handing out gifts. Cook, concerned that Omai might never settle down, finally decided not to leave

The nineteenth-century engraving at right shows a Maori warrior like the ones Cook saw on visits to New Zealand. He described their cloaks as made of dog skins. Some Maori weapons (above) were carved from greenstone jade.

English artists pictured Omai as a swashbuckler: above he poses in a turban; below he shows his horse and his pistol to the Tahitians.

the young native in Tahiti after all. Instead, Omai was taken back to Huahine where he had come from.

The ships' carpenters built him a house. A garden was planted, and some livestock was left for him to tend. Despite these earthly blessings, he died inexplicably within three years. Later, missionaries were quick to assert that Omai had been killed by "inglorious indolence"; perhaps he had been unable to readjust to his primitive culture after a brush with Western civilization.

The calking of seams in the hulls of Cook's ships, and the repairing of masts and sails, delayed the expedition for a time. Cook did not leave the Society Islands until December 8, 1777. Just before Christmas he crossed the equator. He was in the North Pacific for the first time.

At dawn on January 18, 1778, Cook sighted land again —the western islands of the group that was to be called Hawaii. He was the first European ever to see this island group, which he named the Sandwich Islands after the Earl of Sandwich, his patron. Cook did not take time for extensive exploration, but he did observe the people. At first, he noted, they "thought they had a right to anything they could lay their hands upon, but this conduct they soon laid aside." The Hawaiians always traded fairly, moreover, never attempting to cheat, and Cook gradually came to trust them. His stay in Hawaii was altogether pleasurable, but he could not remain there long. An important mission lay ahead of him in northern waters.

On March 7, 1778, he sighted the shores of North America at latitude 44° 30′ (the Oregon coast). His two ships pushed slowly northward, staying close enough to the land to keep it in sight. But soon the *Resolution* was troubled by faults in her masts and rigging. Cook found a deep inlet in Vancouver Island where he remained for most of April. Although he called this inlet King George's Sound, it is known today by its native name, Nootka Sound (see map on page 122). While repairs were being made, the men carried on some trade—mainly in furs—with the Indians, whom Cook described as follows:

Their face is rather broad and flat, with highish cheekbones and plump cheeks. Their mouth is little and round, the nose neither flat nor prominent; their eyes are black, little, and devoid of sparkling fire. But in general they have not a bad shape except in the legs, which in the most of them are crooked and may probably arise from their much sitting. Their complexion is swarthy . . . this seems not altogether natural but proceeds partly from

The Nootka Indians' lodge served as a storehouse for dried fish, a place of worship (note the images along the wall), and a center for their domestic and community life.

smoke, dirt, and paint, for they paint with a liberal hand and are slovenly and dirty to the last degree.

Cook acknowledged that some of the Indians he saw had a certain dignity, but he said their houses were "as filthy as hogsties, everything in and about them stinking of fish, oil, and smoke."

After Vancouver Island, further progress up the west coast of Canada was swift. Careful scrutiny was unnecessary, for the snowy, towering peaks of the coastal ranges suggested that no passage to the east would be found there. Early in May the two ships put in at still another inlet, after a heavy gale had punched leaks into the much-repaired hull of the *Resolution*. Here Cook had his first brush with the Eskimos. They welcomed their visitors with drawn knives and were not afraid when they saw the English firearms. They were eager for booty and were only prevented from using force to obtain it when they realized that Cook's men had longer knives than they had. Thus Cook could boast that his party "had the good fortune to leave [the Eskimos] as ignorant as we found them, for they neither heard nor saw a musket fired unless at birds . . ."

As the ships sailed onward, the coast began to bend in a westerly direction. When Cook saw a break in the land,

129

Masks such as this were worn by members of the Kwakiutl tribe in British Columbia at the time of Cook's visit to the North American coast. They represented supernatural beings and were used in the Kwakiutls' ceremonial dances.

he was certain he had found at last what he had been searching for. His ships had sailed almost a hundred miles into the opening before he realized that he had not found a channel but a sound (Prince William Sound). He would have to search further.

On June 1, Cook entered another deep inlet (Cook Inlet). He did not think this was the sought-after gateway to the northern passage, but he explored it to make sure. Before turning back, Cook reported, he sent two small boats ashore to "take possession of the country and river in His Majesty's name, and to bury in the ground a bottle containing two pieces of English coin (date 1772) and a paper on which was inscribed the ships' names, date, etc."

By the end of June the expedition had passed through the Aleutian Islands and had turned north to follow the Alaska shoreline once again. This part of the voyage was slow and difficult. Fog and wind proved troublesome to navigation, as did the ridges of rock that sometimes ran as far as twenty miles into the sea from the shore. Once, the

TEXT CONTINUED ON PAGE 134

Anchoring in Nootka Sound (below), Cook was greeted by natives offering furs in trade for metal.

After leaving Alaska's south and west coasts, Cook's ships pushed on until they were turned back by the ice floes.

of the Arctic Ocean. Here, one ship sails clear of the ice; the other, temporarily trapped, has furled her sails.

Above is a view of Petropavlovsk, a Russian trading village. It is located on the eastern coast of Asia, where Cook stopped in 1779.

TEXT CONTINUED FROM PAGE 131

Resolution smacked into a sandbank, and the *Discovery* barely avoided following her.

Heading due north, Cook entered Bering Strait. On August 9, 1778, he sighted the westernmost point of North America, which he named Cape Prince of Wales. The next day he crossed the narrowest neck of the strait—only fifty-six miles wide—and landed on the eastern tip of Asia. He was almost as far north as the Arctic Circle. But with cold weather approaching, the farther he sailed the more ice there was to hinder his passage. The best of the summer season had passed.

During the last days of August, Cook steered back and forth—between Asia and America—looking for a break in the ice pack. The search became more difficult as fog and heavy snowfall impaired visibility. Ice clung to the rigging, and the decks had to be continually cleared of snow.

When the ships reached latitude 70°44', the fog lifted momentarily to reveal a wall of ice ten or twelve feet high. This was to mark Cook's farthest north. On August 29, realizing that further penetration was impossible, he decided to direct his ships back to Hawaii and resume his search the following summer. There was nothing more he could do.

On the way south, Cook put in for a time at Unalaska Island, one of the Aleutians. The *Resolution* was again in need of attention. Her sails were in poor condition, her rigging showed signs of wear, and a gale had done fresh damage to her hull. However, because of the approach of cold weather, most of the needed repairs could not be made until the expedition returned to the Hawaiian Islands.

The islands were sighted by late November. For the next eight weeks the ships fought off high winds and bad weather as Cook looked for a safe harbor where his ships might anchor, free from punishing gales. He finally found one in Kealakekua Bay on the west side of Hawaii, biggest island in the group. The ships came to rest as eight hundred native canoes put out from the shore and joyously surrounded both vessels. When Cook at last gave the order to unbend the sails and strike the yards, he noted, "I have nowhere in this sea seen such a number of people assembled in one place. Besides those in the canoes, all the shore of the bay was covered with people, and hundreds were swimming about the ships like shoals of fish."

Neither Cook nor his men understood why they were welcomed back with such ceremony. They could not have known that the native priests had decided Cook was the Hawaiian god of the new year, Rono, who, according to legend, conferred peace and happiness on his subjects. Rono had sailed away from Hawaii many years earlier, the legend went, but before leaving he had prophesied that he would return one day in a great ship carrying a forest of small trees.

Cook had not one but two great ships whose masts looked like trees. He had come now for the second time in less than a year. Thus the islanders assumed that their god had returned to pay them a visit. They brought him gifts, and their chiefs had elaborate ceremonies staged in his honor. He was given a bright red cloak, and the island king himself, old Terreeoboo, placed a feathered helmet on Cook's head. If he enjoyed being revered, that enjoyment was to be short-lived. Soon the natives would treat him as a mortal—and then as a mortal enemy.

RICKMAN, *Journal of Captain Cook,* 1781

This chief of the Unalaskans appears wild and strange, but Cook described these Aleutian Eskimos as being unusually shy and polite.

VII   KEALAKEKUA BAY

136

Two weeks passed, and though the adoration by the native chiefs continued, the enthusiasm of the people began to subside. The chiefs could afford to be generous, for it was the people who supplied the gifts that were lavished daily on the foreign visitors.

Cook did not demand this tribute, but he accepted it. And his sailors, after the months of hardship, could not have refused the bounties that seemed so willingly offered. Fruit, vegetables, coconuts, pigs—all were consumed quickly. When the appetites of the hungry seamen threatened to exhaust the islanders' generosity, one of the lieutenants noted how the natives began "stroking the sides and patting the bellies of the sailors . . . telling them partly by signs and partly by words that it was time for them to go." Finally they did.

In this painting of Honolulu Harbor, done about thirty years after Cook's visits, a jumble of ships' masts is seen at sunset above the peaked roofs of the natives' huts.

On February 4, aware of growing hostility among the people, Cook decided to put out to sea, in the hope of finding another good anchorage farther north. Once again the *Resolution* proved troublesome. Struck by a new gale, the ship's sails were split and her foremast was sprung. She and her consort returned to Kealakekua Bay a week later.

This time their reception was different. No canoes came out to meet them, and when Lieutenant James King led a watering party ashore, he found the islanders both unfriendly and resentful. As he was being rowed back to the *Resolution* he saw a native canoe paddling away from the *Discovery*. He learned later that as Captain Clerke was entertaining a chief in his cabin a thief had climbed up the side of the ship. The thief had run across the deck in full view of everyone present, snatched the armorer's chisel and tongs, and jumped overboard into a waiting canoe.

The incident was reported at once to Cook. He sent a pinnace, under the command of Midshipman Vancouver and Mr. Edgar, sailing master of the *Discovery*, to recover the stolen tools and seize the thief. After some argument with the natives, Edgar succeeded in retrieving the tongs and chisel, but the thief had vanished. As a reprisal, Edgar seized a native canoe that was drawn up on the beach. The owner of the boat, a young chief named Parea, appeared on the scene at that moment to protect his property.

In the scuffle that followed, Parea was struck on the head with an oar; Edgar was attacked and soundly beaten; and Vancouver was knocked down when he tried to intervene. A shower of stones forced the Englishmen to swim out to a rock a short distance from shore. Their pinnace was left unguarded. The natives immediately swarmed into it, removing whatever articles they could find—even Vancouver's cap. They would have demolished the boat entirely if Parea had not recovered from his blow in time to drive them off. The Englishmen swam back to shore, and Parea, fearful that Rono might kill him for starting the disturbance, begged Edgar's forgiveness.

When Cook learned of the episode, he was furious. He blamed Edgar for mishandling the affair and for becoming embroiled in a dangerous quarrel. The priests, it was clear, might still be on the strangers' side, but the temper of the islanders clearly was rising. "I am afraid," said Cook, "that these people will oblige me to use some violent measures, for they must not be left to imagine they have gained an advantage over us."

This attitude was sound, for it was essential that Cook's

Louis Choris painted the Hawaiian portraits at right: two young men in native garb and a king with a strangely transparent crown. Below is a sketch of a feast the Hawaiians gave to honor Cook. The man who is presenting food to the Englishman is a chief named Koah.

prestige, if not his supposed divinity, be maintained. Some-
one suggested that there might be strong native resistance
to any attempt at retribution, but Cook insisted, "They
will not stand the fire of a single musket." He was certain
that his men could suppress the populace just by firing a
shot or two.

At daybreak the next morning, February 14, it was
learned that the *Discovery*'s cutter had been stolen during
the night. As far as Cook was concerned, "violent measures" were now in order. He decided to follow a practice
that had always been successful in cases of serious theft:
to take an important hostage until the stolen article was
returned. He armed his marines and loaded his double-
barreled musket—one barrel with small shot to scatter a
crowd, the other with ball to kill.

Two boats were rowed ashore. Aboard were Cook and
a contingent of nine marines commanded by Lieutenant
Molesworth Phillips. A third boat was sent to the other
side of the bay to prevent the natives from organizing a
canoe-borne counterattack. The climactic hour of Cook's
career was at hand. Lieutenant Phillips, in his report
to Captain Clerke, recorded everything that took place
in that brief but crucial span of time.

As soon as Cook landed, he made his way to the village
of King Terreeoboo. A short talk proved that Terreeoboo
knew nothing about the theft of the cutter. But Cook wished
to speak with him further and proposed that they return
to the *Resolution* and spend the day together. Terreeoboo
agreed to go, but the crowd of natives that had gathered
outside his hut protested loudly. They told the king that
Cook would surely kill him, and they appeared determined
to keep him from going.

Phillips ordered the marines to make a lane through
the crowd all the way to the beach. Cook and his hostage
passed easily through the lane, but when they were in sight
of the boats a woman broke through the cordon and begged
the king not to go. She was, it seemed, his favorite wife. As
she threw her arms around her husband, the mob surged
forward, pressing the marines so close that they could not
fire their muskets. Phillips sensed that the situation was becoming dangerous. He asked Cook if the men should be
drawn up close to the water's edge to secure a retreat. Cook
replied coolly that there was no real danger but that Phillips could do as he wished. So the marines formed a line
along the shore, standing with their backs to the sea.

Cook stood some twenty-five yards away from the

In this dramatic painting of the natives' assault on Cook, the explorer is shown swinging the butt of his discharged musket. One of the Hawaiians is preparing to hurl a rock with a sling; another stabs Cook. If the pinnaces had been as close to shore as pictured here, Cook might have been rescued.

141

beach, trying to persuade the king to ignore his wife's entreaties and go aboard the *Resolution*. The old man was sitting on the ground looking frightened and dejected, and every time he made a move to follow Cook, the chiefs stopped him. One of them tried to hit Cook in the face with a breadfruit. Another was about to hurl a stone when a fellow native restrained his arm.

Cook was ready to give up trying to take the king and order a withdrawal from the beach when a native runner burst through the crowd. He relayed the news that the Eng-

lish party on the other side of the bay had fired on a canoe and killed an important chief. This shocked the mob into action. The men began putting on their matlike war cloaks, and many stooped to gather handfuls of stones. Others shook their clubs and spears fiercely.

The situation was now as dangerous as Phillips had imagined it would be, and Cook finally realized it. He and Phillips started walking down to the water as the Hawaiians' shouts grew louder and angrier.

An islander came menacingly near, brandishing an iron

spike and a sharp stone. Cook faced about in time to fire a charge of small shot, which made no impression on the assailant's thick cloak. He fired at the man again—this time discharging ball—and killed another islander instead. Retaliating, the natives began to march on the line of marines, filling the air with a rain of stones.

The marines fired a volley, which halted the rioters, but only for a moment. They continued to advance while the muskets were being reloaded—an operation that took several moments. During the interval, Cook was seen making his way down to the beach, shouting to the boats to pull in closer. One boat came very near the rocks offshore but was still several yards from the beach. It would have taken only a few minutes for Cook to wade out and be pulled aboard, but it was too late. In a moment he was surrounded.

One native struck him from behind with a club, and he fell on his knees. Another stabbed him between the shoulders with a dagger, and he sprawled face down into the

In command after Cook's death, Clerke continued the search for a northern passage. Here his ships put in for supplies at a Russian post on Kamchatka.

A tree stump near the place of Cook's death was sketched by an American artist visiting Kealakekua Bay in the early 1800's.

shallow water at the sea's edge. A great shout arose, and the crowd flung itself on the captain's body, stabbing in a frenzy of blood lust.

It was all over quickly. Four marines were killed beside Cook on the beach, and the rest scrambled for the nearest boat. Phillips, who had been wounded himself by this time, was unable to swim, yet he jumped out to help one of his men aboard. Once both boats were out of the way, the big guns of the *Discovery* and the *Resolution* soon cleared the beach of natives, but by then Cook's body had been dragged away. "When we saw his blood running and heard his groans," so ran a Hawaiian legend, "we said, 'This is not Rono.'"

Only an hour had passed since Cook and the marines had gone ashore. And now Cook was dead. He was fifty years old and had been as hardy as ever, but his career was over. It was hard to believe. On both the *Resolution* and the *Discovery* the men were quiet that day. Phillips wrote that he could not put into words how the loss of Cook was lamented; "Much less," he said, "shall I attempt to paint the horror with which we were struck and the universal dejection which followed so dreadful . . . a calamity."

The Hawaiians too felt mournful—and repentant—soon after the episode was over. They had grown to respect Cook aside from their belief that he was one of their gods. His body was placed on a burning pyre and accorded funeral rites that were usually reserved for the most revered of heroes.

Two days after Cook's death, a native who had shown himself to be a friend of the English went to the *Resolution* and delivered a bundle. It was wrapped in fine new cloth and covered with a cloak of black and white feathers. Inside was all that was left of Captain James Cook.

The remains were placed in a coffin, and at sunset on February 21, as the ships' guns boomed a ten-minute salute, the coffin was committed to the deep. "We all felt we had lost a father," was the reaction of one seaman, whose sentiment typified that of his fellows. Even the Hawaiian king, Terreeoboo, mourned the death of the English captain, right along with the crew.

Clerke was now the leader of the expedition. It was his task to complete the voyage and take the ships home. His health was not good, however, for he had been afflicted with tuberculosis even before he had left England. The disease had advanced significantly, but he could not begin the homeward voyage yet. He felt compelled to complete

145

In 1784, Mrs. Cook received the gold medal above from the Royal Society in honor of her husband's work. Dignified in her widowhood (below), she died at ninety-three.

what Cook had started and to try, if possible, to locate the northern passage. The day after Cook's funeral, Clerke ordered the two ships to weigh anchor. He took command of the *Resolution* and assigned the *Discovery* to Gore.

Sailing northwest toward Asia, the voyagers sighted the Kamchatka peninsula on April 23, and at the harbor of St. Peter and St. Paul (now called Petropavlovsk) they were received cordially by the Russians. They even did some trading in furs. Despite language differences, Clerke managed to convey to his hosts that he wished to send a letter home by land. The letter was eventually delivered to the Admiralty, and England learned of the disaster in Kealakekua Bay eight months before the voyage ended.

On June 13 the ships began their second northward push along the Asiatic coast. Dense fog and the thickening ice floes made sailing hazardous and slow—and ultimately impossible. When the *Resolution* and the *Discovery* were fifteen miles short of the point reached on the first attempt, they were stopped. Clerke realized the hopelessness of sailing farther, as well as the seriousness of his own affliction. He was growing weaker daily. On July 27 he turned his ships back; he had no choice.

In less than a month Clerke was dead. He was buried at Petropavlovsk where the ships dropped anchor on August 24. Now John Gore assumed command of the *Resolution*, and James King took over the *Discovery*.

Gore wanted to sail south along the Japanese coast and survey as much of it as possible. But foul weather prevented this. Savage winds split the worn-out sails of both ships and cut the rotten cordage. Driven away from the shore, the ships ran directly to the European settlement at Macao, where they dropped anchor on December 1, 1779.

While the *Resolution* and the *Discovery* were being refitted, their crews turned a handsome profit trading the furs they had on board with the Chinese, who eagerly bought them. This was a portent, for the fur trade between North America and China would soon be enormous.

In Macao, where they could read European newspapers, Gore and King learned that England's war with her American colonies was not going well. By this time France had entered the conflict against the English, but French and American ships had been ordered not to molest the vessels of the Cook expedition. However, Gore was experienced enough in war to realize the necessity of bringing guns up from the holds. He made sure the ships' companies were prepared for any emergency as they swept around the

SIR T. BROCK R.A.
SCULP. 1914

London's famous statue of Cook, standing beyond Admiralty Arch, is a monument to the man, to an era, and to English naval history.

147

Cape of Good Hope and sailed into the North Atlantic. As a further safeguard, Gore altered his course to the west to avoid the European coast. He was taking no chances on an encounter with the French. After such a long period at sea, neither of his ships was in fighting trim; nor had they the speed to evade pursuit. Gore guided them around Ireland and Scotland before approaching his final anchorage at Deptford on October 6, 1780.

The voyage had lasted four years and almost three months. During that time the *Resolution* had lost only four men from illness; three of them—Clerke included—had not been in good health when the voyage began. The *Discovery* returned with her crew intact. By continuing to enforce the dietary discipline initiated by Cook, the officers who succeeded him had maintained the crews' good health. Cook had shown that scurvy need not be a major problem on long voyages. He had not succeeded by cajolery, for he did not impress men by a display of charm. Men trusted him because of the example he set and because of his sense of responsibility and his unshakable confidence.

His self-confidence and his certainty that the natives could be subdued by threats of force betrayed him in the end. But by then his work was finished. In eleven years of geographical discovery he had proved that the Pacific was more vast and more varied than most geographers had imagined. He had shown that the unknown southern continent, if it existed, lay too far south to support life. And his foray in the North proved that there was no practicable northern passage through which ships of trade might sail. Another voyage could have told him little that he did not already know or imagine.

The explorers who followed him did not diminish the stature of his achievements. They amplified what he had done, but no one ever surpassed his record. From South America to Australia, from the ice islands of the South Pacific to the fogbound Bering Strait, lay thousands of miles of islands, atolls, and ocean that Cook had charted.

Curiosity made Cook an explorer. Zeal and resolution kept him at his tasks and helped him surmount all obstacles. Precision insured that what he saw was fully and accurately recorded. These were the qualities that made up the man. His legacy was knowledge; his monument is the map of the Pacific.

Tahiti's natural beauty has not diminished in the years since Cook's time.

149

Cook was honored in folk art as well as in fine art. This Staffordshire teapot bears an allegorical scene of Cook, holding his commission, at Britannia's knee.

ACKNOWLEDGMENTS

AMERICAN HERITAGE PUBLISHING CO., INC.

James Parton, *President*

Joseph J. Thorndike, Jr., *Editorial Director*

Richard M. Ketchum, *Editor, Book Division*

Irwin Glusker, *Art Director*

HORIZON CARAVEL BOOKS

RUSSELL BOURNE, *Managing Editor*

Janet Czarnetzki, *Art Director*

Mervyn Kaufman, *Associate Editor*

Judith Harkison, *Chief Picture Researcher*

Lucy Davidson Rosenfeld, *Picture Researcher*

Elaine K. Andrews, *Copy Editor*

Mary Gloyne Payne, *Editorial Assistant*

Nancy Simon, *Editorial Assistant*

Gertrudis Feliu, *Chief, European Bureau*

The Editors are deeply grateful to the curators and staff members of the many private and public collections in Australia, New Zealand, England, and the United States in which paintings, charts, and exploration journals of special value to this book were found. Special thanks are owed to A. A. Murray-Oliver of The Alexander Turnbull Library in Wellington, New Zealand, the staff and R. S. Skelton, Keeper of the Map Division of the British Museum, and Mrs. Marjorie Hancock of The Mitchell Library in Sydney, Australia. In addition the Editors wish to thank the following individuals and organizations for their assistance:

C. Preston, Whitby Literary and Philosophical Society, Yorkshire
Etienne Taillemite, Archives Nationales, Paris
Agnes Beriot, Paris
Mrs. E. Cole, Rare Book Division, New York Public Library
Mrs. Fritz Hart, Honolulu Academy of Arts
H. L. White, National Library of Australia, Canberra
Mlles. Foncin and de la Ronciere, Map Division, Bibliothèque Nationale
S. B. Maclennan, National Art Gallery, Wellington
O. P. Gabites, Consul General, and Michael Robson of the New Zealand Consulate General, New York
Elizabeth Little, The Museum of Primitive Art, New York
Mrs. G. Kenneth Stout, Wellesley Hills, Mass.
Staff of the Manuscript Division, British Museum

Special research and photography: New York—Geoffrey Clements, Zoltan Wegner, and Derek Bayes; London—Susanne Puddefoot

Maps by Herbert Borst

FURTHER REFERENCE

Readers who are interested in further exploring the Pacific through its primitive art and natural history will find collections in many American cities. Outstanding among the museums displaying objects from the area are The Museum of Primitive Art and the American Museum of Natural History, New York City; the University of California, T. Wayland Vaughan Aquarium Museum, La Jolla; the Bernice P. Bishop Museum, Honolulu; the Denver Art Museum; the Milwaukee Public Museum; the Alaska Historical Library and Museum, Juneau; the Sheldon Jackson Junior College Museum, Sitka; the United States Department of the Interior Museum; and the Museum of History and Industry, Seattle. Collections dealing more particularly with Captain Cook and the history of exploration can be found at The Mariners Museum, Newport News; the Marine Historical Association, Inc., Mystic, Conn.; the Peabody Museum, Salem; the Massachusetts Institute of Technology, Francis Russell Hart Nautical Museum, Cambridge; the New York Public Library, Rare Book Division; the San Francisco Maritime Museum; the California State Library, Sutro; and the Honolulu Academy of Arts.

For those who wish to read more about Captain Cook and the South Pacific, the following books are recommended:

Beaglehole, J. C. *The Exploration of the Pacific*. A. & C. Black Ltd., 1934.

Beaglehole, J. C., ed. *The Journals of Captain Cook*, Vol. I, *The Voyage of the Endeavour 1768–1771*. Cambridge University Press, 1955. Vol. II, *The Voyage of the Resolution and the Adventure 1772–1775*. Cambridge University Press, 1961.

Birket-Smith, Kaj. *Primitive Man and his Ways*. World Publishing Co., 1960.

Bligh, William. *The Mutiny on Board H.M.S. Bounty*. Signet Classic, 1962.

Buck, Peter H. *Vikings of the Pacific*. University of Chicago Press, 1959.

Buehler, Alfred, et al. *The Arts of the South Sea Islands*. Crown Publishers, Inc., 1962.

Fraser, Douglas. *Primitive Art*. Doubleday, 1962.

Heyerdahl, Thor. *Kon-Tiki*. Rand McNally, 1950.

Judd, Gerrit P. *Hawaii, An Informal History*. Collier Books, 1961.

Kippis, Andrew. *Captain Cook's Voyages*. Knopf, 1924.

Linton, Ralph and Wingert, Paul S. *Arts of the South Seas*. Museum of Modern Art, 1946.

Nowell, Charles, ed. *Magellan's Voyage Around the World. Three Contemporary Accounts*. Northwestern University Press, 1962.

Price, A. Grenfell, ed. *The Explorations of Captain James Cook in the Pacific*. The Heritage Press.

Rowe, Newton A. *Voyage to the Amorous Islands*. Andre Deutsch, 1955.

Sharp, Andrew. *Ancient Voyagers in the Pacific*. Penguin Books Ltd., 1957.

Skelton, R. A. *Explorers' Maps*. Praeger, 1958.

Wingert, Paul *Primitive Art, Its Tradition and Styles*. Oxford University Press, 1962.

INDEX

Bold face indicates pages on which maps or illustrations appear

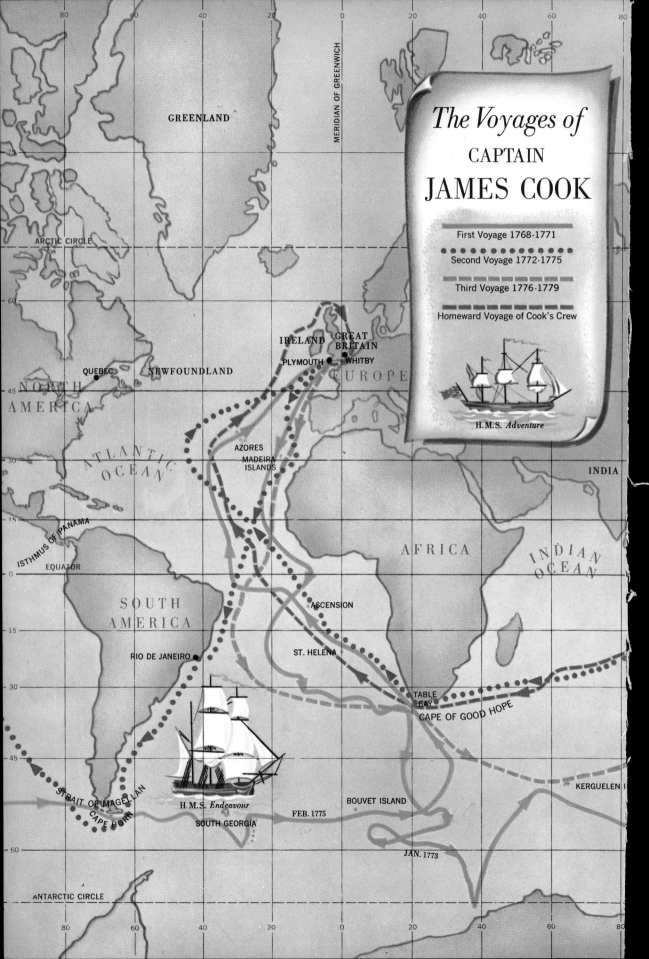

The Voyages of
CAPTAIN
JAMES COOK

First Voyage 1768-1771
Second Voyage 1772-1775
Third Voyage 1776-1779
Homeward Voyage of Cook's Crew

H.M.S. *Adventure*

GREENLAND

MERIDIAN OF GREENWICH

ARCTIC CIRCLE

IRELAND   GREAT BRITAIN
PLYMOUTH ●   ● WHITBY
QUEBEC ●   NEWFOUNDLAND   EUROPE

NORTH AMERICA

ATLANTIC OCEAN

AZORES
MADEIRA ISLANDS

INDIA

AFRICA

INDIAN OCEAN

ISTHMUS OF PANAMA
EQUATOR

ASCENSION

SOUTH AMERICA

RIO DE JANEIRO ●   ST. HELENA

TABLE BAY
CAPE OF GOOD HOPE

H.M.S. *Endeavour*

STRAIT OF MAGELLAN
CAPE HORN

KERGUELEN I

BOUVET ISLAND
FEB. 1775
SOUTH GEORGIA

JAN. 1773

ANTARCTIC CIRCLE